TEAM HANDBALL
Skills, Strategies and Training

Baha M. Hamil
and
James D. LaPoint

D1531500

eddie bowers publishing, inc.
2600 Jackson Street
Dubuque, Iowa 52001-3342

eddie bowers publishing, inc.
2600 Jackson Street
Dubuque, Iowa 52001

ISBN 0-945483-23-6

Copyright © 1994, by *eddie bowers publishing, inc.*

Printed in the United States of America.

9 8 7 6 5 4 3 2 1

DEDICATION

This book is dedicated to our wives and families. In addition, we would like to thank our parents for their support in helping us understand the true value of sport and its merits for promoting a fuller appreciation of a healthy life-style.

ACKNOWLEDGMENTS

The authors would like to thank the following people for their valuable contributions to the book: Dr. Peter G. Buehning, President and Founder of the United States Team Handball Federation; Michael Cavanaugh, Executive Director of the USTHF; Vojtech Mares, Head Coach, United States Men's National Team; Rick Oleksyk, Men's Coach, United States Men's National Team; Dr. Wayne Osness, Chairman of the HPER Department at the University of Kansas and member of the United States Olympic Committee; Allen Heinze, Director of Facilities for Robinson Center at the University of Kansas; Mary Chappel, Director of the University of Kansas Recreational Sports Services; Gordon Kratz, Director of Sports Clubs at the University of Kansas; University of Kansas Team Handball Club; Darcy Maddox, typist; and Patricia Lee Drewry, illustrator.

CONTENTS   iii

PREFACE

Team Handball: Skills, Strategies and Training is a text book that has been written to satisfy two diverse audiences. Since this is the first book published on team handball in the past 20 years, there are a substantial number of people who have never been formally introduced to this exciting international sport. At the other end of the spectrum, are the players and coaches who have been looking, without success, for a book that deals with team handball as a serious Olympic sport.

The book covers all aspects of team handball, beginning with the basic fundamentals, advanced skills, and advanced strategies.

The game of team handball has seen a slow but steady growth over the past five to seven years. The major difficulty faced by this sport is the lack of national recognition. Even with the 1984 Olympics held in the United States of America, television coverage was minimal at best. The growth has emerged at the local club level, as well as in the schools where the physical education teachers have introduced the game as a new activity to students at all levels, elementary through high school. The American colleges have been equally slow in initiating Team Handball classes for the college students.

The most positive aspect of team handball is that in this same time period, the United States Team Handball Federation introduced the formal training of players at the Olympic Training Center in Colorado Springs, Colorado. This organization has taken a very active role in this process of selecting elite team handball players to represent the United States.

No matter what the level of play, or the aspiration of the player, team handball is a game of combining and utilizing simple motor skills of running, catching, throwing, jumping, and shooting. This book considers all of the components of the game that lead to the development of the accomplished player. The book is assembled in the same way a coach typically approaches the coaching of a competitive sport. It starts with the basics of body position, mechanics of holding the ball, passing, shooting, offensive and defensive patterns, strategy, and rules of the game. The book is designed to be used for all levels of teaching and coaching Team Handball.

CONTENTS

Chapter 3
Basic Playing Strategies

Chapter 4
Defensive Strategies

Chapter 5
Offensive Strategies   79

GRAPHIC SYMBOLS LEGEND

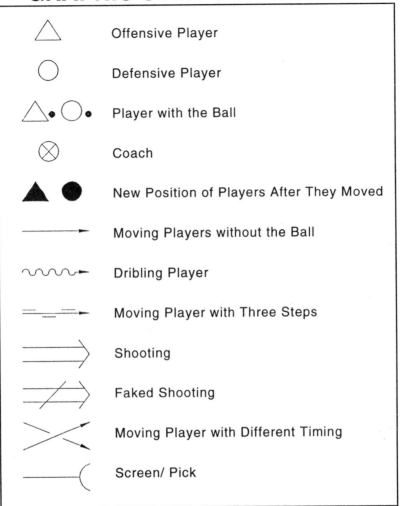

△	Offensive Player
○	Defensive Player
△• ○•	Player with the Ball
⊗	Coach
▲ ●	New Position of Players After They Moved
──────►	Moving Players without the Ball
∿∿∿►	Dribling Player
══════►	Moving Player with Three Steps
═════▷	Shooting
═════▷	Faked Shooting
✕	Moving Player with Different Timing
─────(	Screen/ Pick

METRIC CONVERSION VALUES

1 inch = 2.54 Centimeters (CM)

1 foot = 30.48 Centimeters (CM)

1 yard = .9144 Meters (M)

TEAM HANDBALL   Skills, Strategies and Training

INTRODUCTION TO TEAM HANDBALL

HISTORY

The beginnings of Team Handball are somewhat vague. It appears that it originated around the turn of the century in several European countries as different variations of the same sport. In Denmark, a team handball program was started for gymnastic students in 1898 by Halger Nelson. He wrote a booklet about his game in 1907, calling this sport "Hambald." In Czechoslovakia in 1892 a similar game, known as "Hazena," was played on a soccer field with 11 players. By 1905, Hazena was played with seven players. A few years later team handball was played in Switzerland with the same basic rules. The game appears in the USSR in 1910 and in Sweden in 1919. The first team handball game reported in the United States was in 1919 in Los Angeles. The sport was reportedly brought here by a new immigrant.

It was in Germany that the team handball game closest to what is played today was developed. In 1917, Max Heiser developed the game which he called "handball," as part of a physical conditioning program for women gymnasts. This game was played with seven players on an indoor court which was 20 X 40 meters in size. It has two goals, each with a four meter radius goal area. The rules were a combination of rules from sports such as "raffball," "korbballspiel" and soccer (football). Physical contact and running with the ball were restricted in these games.

Team handball began as a sport played with 11 players on an outdoor soccer field and gradually changed to a game with seven players, usually played on an indoor court. This change in team size produced a faster, more exciting game for both players and spectators. In the development of team handball, the ball size was also reduced to increase the speed of the game. Team handball was first played with a soccer or similar-sized ball that had to be thrown like a discus. With a smaller ball that could be gripped in the palm, players could use shoulder, arm, and wrist action to propel the ball, increasing the accuracy and speed of their throw. This also changed team handball from a running and jumping game to one in which passing became an important part of team strategy. The rules gradually changed to allow for more physical contact and running with the ball, adding more action to the game.

During the 1920's team handball increased in popularity. Many tournaments were held for men and women throughout Europe and other parts of the world. The International Team Handball Federation (IHF) was founded in 1928 with headquarters in Berlin. Membership included 11 countries: Canada, Czechoslovakia, Denmark, Finland, France, Germany, Greece, Ireland, Norway, Sweden and United States. They set up the modern rules for team handball. By the 1930's membership in the International Team Handball Federation had expanded to include the majority of European nations, Argentina, Brazil, Iceland, Japan, Haiti and Egypt. It had become one of the most popular spectator sports in Germany, Norway, Sweden, Denmark, Holland and Japan.

ORGANIZATION

The United States Team Handball Federation (USTHF) conducts the International Team Handball program of the United States of America. In addition, it serves as the national governing body, directing the United States Team Handball program for the Olympic Games. The USTHF is also responsible for developing the national teams for women, men, and juniors and for administering the regulations of the International Handball Federation (IHF). The USTHF is also responsible for selecting teams to represent the United States in the Pan American Games and the Goodwill Games.

The following chronology will help to give some perspective on the game's development:

1904	Originated in European Countries
1915	Women's sport in Germany
1920	Berlin Athletic Union adopted Team Handball as a sport
1921	First German National Team Handball championships
1924	First international rules were adopted
1928	ITHF was established as the governing body of Team Handball
1934	Meeting of the ITHF. Established amateur Team Handball as an indoor activity (Prior to this, Team Handball had only been an outdoor activity)
1936	Team Handball established as an Olympic sport
1946	IHF formed; ITHF dissolved
1959	USTHF founded in New York
1960	League play in New York New Jersey area with eight teams
1962	USTHF becomes a member of IHF
1964	US. National Team participates for the first time in the World Team Handball Championships
1968	USTHF becomes a member of the US. Olympic Committee
1971	Beginning of US. Army Team Handball promotion and development program
1972	Team Handball as a men's sport in the Munich Olympics. (US. Men's Team participated and finished 14th place)
1976	Team Handball as a women's sport in the Montreal Olympics. (US. Men's Team participated and finished 10th place)
1979	Team Handball moved its operations to Olympic Training Center in Colorado Springs, CO for full-time training and development
1980	US. National Team Men and Women did not qualify for the Olympics
1984	USA finished ninth in the Los Angeles Olympics (Men)
1986	USA finished second in the Goodwill Games (Men)
1987	USA finished first in the Pan American Games (Men)
1987	USA finished first in the Pan American Games (Women)
1988	USA finished twelfth in the Seoul Olympics (Men)
1988	USA finished seventh in the Seoul Olympics (Women)
1989	USA finished second in the Pan American Championships (Women)
1989	USA finished third in the Pan American Games (Men)
1990	USA finished fourth in the Goodwill Games (Men)
1991	USA finished third in the Pan American Games (Men)
1991	USA finished first in the Pan American Championships (Women)
1992	USA finished sixth in Barcelona Olympics (Women)

THE GAME OF TEAM HANDBALL

Team handball is a game that can be played by both men and women. It is a sport which combines the skills of *running, jumping, catching, and throwing* into a fast-moving, exciting game. The game is usually played with seven players on each team, however, under some modifications, it can be played with as few as five players. Elements of such diverse sports as soccer, basketball, hockey, and water polo are seen in the skills needed to play team handball. The basic objective of the game is to outmaneuver the opponent by passing and dribbling the ball quickly and then to throwing the ball past the defense and the goalie to score. Each goal counts one point for the scoring team. The team scoring the most goals in the time allotted wins the game.

Team handball is a simple game, easily played and enjoyed at first attempts by players of any age. The rapid continuous play, spectacular leaps and dives into the air by players attempting to score and the quick reactions of the goalie make the game enjoyable for spectators as well as players.

All court lines in team handball are referred to by their measurement in meters. The most significant line on the court is the *6 meter line*, or *goal area line*. The area enclosed by the 6 meter line is called the goal area or the "circle." Only the goalie is allowed to stand inside the goal area. However, an offensive or defensive player may be in the air above the circle and land in the circle as long as their take-off was from outside of the goal area line. The player cannot interfere with play in any way after landing in the goal area and must exit by the shortest route possible.

The *9 meter line*, also called the *free throw line*, is used for minor penalties in the game. The fouls and penalties that occur between the 6 and 9 meter lines are always brought back outside the 9 meter line for a restart of the game. The *7 meter line*, or *penalty line*, is used for a major penalty. Any of the players on the floor from the offended team shoots one-on-one against the goalie. In this type of situation, the shooter has a distinct advantage, and the probability of scoring a goal is very high.

The regulation court is larger than a basketball court, 20 x 40 meters (65 ft. x 131 ft.), but the game can be easily adapted to a smaller area. The width of the court is more important than the length. Many

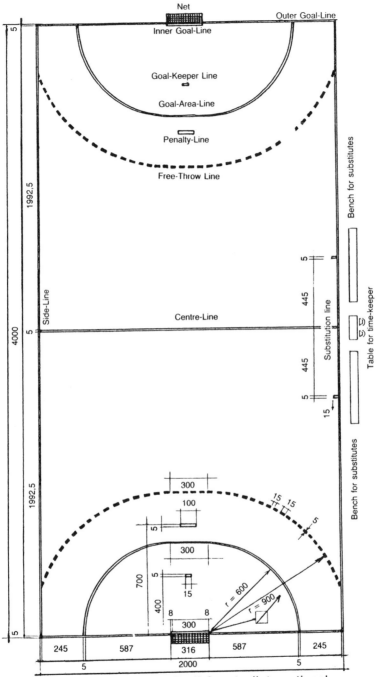

Figure 1.1   Team Handball Court   (International Measurements are based on the Metric System.)

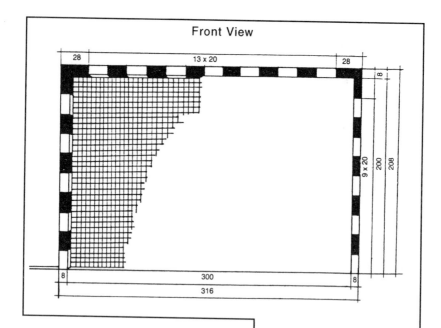

Front View

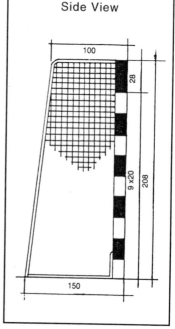

Side View

of the younger players will start in an elementary school in a physical education gymnasium and work their way up to larger courts as they get older (See figure 1.1).

The goals are 2 x 3 meters (6 ft. 7 in. high x 10 ft. wide). Goals can be purchased or made. The goal is provided with a net to prevent the rebound of the ball off the back area. If at all possible, the goal should be secured to the ground or floor (See figure 1.2).

The ball varies in size and weight depending upon the group participating in the game. The adult men's ball is 58-60 cm (23 in) in circumference, and weighs about 425-475 grams (16-17oz.). Women,

Figure 1.2   Goal

teenagers, and children use a smaller ball, about 54-56 cm (21 in) in circumference and weighing about 325-400 grams (15-16 oz.). There is also a smaller mini-handball for younger players which is 48-50 cm (19 in) in circumference. The ball looks like a small soccer ball. It has a rubber bladder inside a leather cover. Several sporting goods companies have put out new mini-balls with softer spongier coverings. These are especially effective in allowing the younger players to grasp the ball cleanly before starting to pass or shoot. The newer softer balls have also helped younger players, particularly those playing the goalie position, to stay in their positions without having to worry about being hit with the heavier leather ball.

DURATION OF THE GAME

According to IHF rules, playing time is two 30-minute halves with a 10-minute intermission. There are no time outs except for injuries or other major interruptions, as determined by the referees. Playing time can be modified for tournaments and younger players. For example, the USTHF has set two 20-minute periods with 10-minute intermission for regular tournament games; in some tournaments when time and space are limited, two 10-minute periods with a 5-minute intermission. For male juniors, playing time is two 25-minute periods with an intermission of 10-minutes; in tournaments, two 10-minute periods with no intermission.

Before the game begins, the coaches and the referee decide whether or not the game can end in a tie. If it is decided to play until a winner is determined and a tie exists at the end of regulation time, there is a provision for overtime consisting of two 5-minute periods. Teams have a five minute interval, then a coin toss determines who will have the throw-off or choice of ends in the overtime period. Teams change ends at half time with no interval. If the game is still tied at the end of the overtime, the teams have a five minute interval and play a second period of overtime after a second coin toss. If the game is still tied after the second period of overtime, the rules of the competition will be applied to determine the winner (see the IHF Rules).

THE PLAYERS

According to IHF Rules, each official team is composed of 12 players; 10 court players and 2 goalies. Only 6 court players and 1 goalie play at one time. The designated positions are goalkeeper (G), circle runner (CR), right wing (RW), left wing (LW), right back (RB), left back (LB), and center back (CB). Since players are permitted to move freely about the court there are no rules regulating the positions of the court players (See figure 1.3).

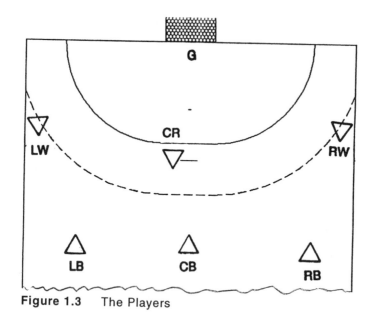

Figure 1.3   The Players

Substitutions are made from the bench area near the mid court line. A substitute may enter the game when the court player has left the playing area. The incoming substitute does not need to notify the timekeeper. The substitution procedure for the goalkeeper is the same as for the court players, however, the new goalie must have a jersey which is distinctive in color from other court players. Illegal substitution may result in a free throw or penalty throw for the opponent.

ÆUGSBURG
C · O · L · L · E · G · E

Library

FINES POLICY

Augsburg College Library items not returned within one month of the due date will be billed a $50 lost charge. $40 of this may be refunded if the item is later returned. The remaining $10 processing fee is non-refundable. Past-due items borrowed from other libraries may be assessed non-refundable fines, depending upon the policies of the loaning library. Payment of all fines is made through the Augsburg College Business Office.

Due date for this material:

Jan	1	11	21
Feb	2	12	22
Mar	3	13	23
Apr	4	14	24
May	5	15	25
Jun	6	16	26
Jul	7	17	27
Aug	8	18	28
Sep	9	19	29
Oct	10	20	30
Nov			31
Dec			

ÆUGSBURG
C·O·L·L·E·G·E

Library

Circulation: 330-1017
Reference: 330-1604
http://www.augsburg.edu/library

LIBRARY HOURS:

Mon-Fri	8 a.m. - 11 p.m.
Saturday	8 a.m. - 6 p.m.
Sunday	Noon - 11 p.m.

Hours vary during summer, holidays and finals week.

I.D. CARDS

All Augsburg students, staf
faculty, and CLIC patrons mu
show a current I.D. card in
order to check out materials.
Alumni and friends must sho
a picture I.D. to apply for a
library card. In addition, all
friends will be asked to pay
$10/item fee upon checkout,
which is refunded when the
books are returned.

BORROWING ITEMS

Books are charged out at th
circulation desk and are due i
six weeks. Books charged to
faculty and staff circulate for
one term. Reference books,
periodicals, and microfilm do
not circulate.

COURT PLAYERS' PLAYING PRIVILEGES

1. A player is allowed to run 3 steps with the ball or hold it for 3 seconds. A player is not allowed to play the ball with the legs below the knee. There is no limit on dribbling the ball, however, a double dribble (dribbling, pausing, then dribbling again) is not permitted and a free throw is awarded to the opponent. In summary, a player may:
    *   take 3 steps
    *   dribble (as long as desired)
    *   take 3 steps
    *   then pass or shoot within 3 seconds
2. A player may not pass the ball into the air with the intention of catching it while advancing down the court. This is called an air dribble and it is not legal. Players other than the goalkeeper are not permitted to dive for the ball when it is lying or rolling on the floor.
3. While in the act of defense, a player is allowed to use the body to obstruct the offensive player, whether the offensive player has or does not possess the ball. However, using the arms or legs to obstruct, push, hold, trip, or hit is not allowed. The offensive player is not allowed to charge into a defensive player. A free throw is awarded if this occurs. The ball must be the object of attack by the defensive player at all times.
4. Stalling is not permitted by either team. (This is a referee's judgement call).
5. Players may be suspended from play for 2 minutes, or permanently, depending on the severity of the foul.

GOALKEEPER PLAYING PRIVILEGES

1. The goalkeeper may defend the goal in any manner using the hands, feet, or any other part of the body. The goalie may wear gloves and padded shirts and shorts for protection, similar to those worn by a soccer goalkeeper. The goalkeeper is not permitted to wear a mask or a chest protector.
2. When the goalie has possession of the ball outside the goal area, all rules that apply to court players are in effect.

3. The goalie is free to move outside the goal area anytime without the ball, but must then abide by the rules for other court players. The goalkeeper then becomes the seventh court player, leaving the team without a goalkeeper.

4. The goalkeeper is not permitted to leave the goal area while in possession of the ball. (Penalty: a free throw is awarded to the other team when this occurs.)

5. The goalkeeper is prohibited from picking up a loose ball outside the 6 meter line and carrying it back into the goal area unless the ball is bouncing. (Penalty: a penalty throw will be awarded to the other team when this occurs.)

6. When the goalkeeper recovers a blocked or missed shot and attempts a throw-out from inside the circle, opponents can block the throw from outside the 6 meter line. If the blocked shot rebounds back into the goal, a score will result.

7. A court player substituted for a goalkeeper must notify the referee before entering the goal area (penalty: penalty throw). This court player cannot enter the goal area until the goalkeeper is off the court (penalty: penalty throw).

8. The court players are not permitted to throw the ball back to their own goalie to take the pressure off their team while the goalkeeper is still inside the goal area (penalty: penalty shot).

START OF PLAY

An official game begins with each team having, at most, six court players and one designated goalkeeper on the floor. The referee holds a coin toss for the team captains. The winning captain chooses between having the throw off or choice of ends. Once everyone is ready, the referee blows the whistle and the offensive team has 3 seconds to put the ball into play. At the start, all players must be on their own half of the court. The defensive players must be at least 3 meters (10 ft.) back from the ball. A goal can be scored directly from a throw-off.

When taking a throw-off, throw-in, free-throw, or penalty throw, the player making the throw must keep part of one foot in constant contact with the ground or floor until the ball is released. The player is permitted, however, to lift the other foot in any manner.

BALL OUT OF BOUNDS

A ball is considered to be out of bounds when the entire ball has crossed the goal line (See figure 1.4) or sideline (See figure 1.5). A ball crossing the sideline is put back into play with a throw-in by the team that did not last touch the ball before it went out of bounds. A throw-in is executed from outside the sidelines, with one foot remaining on the floor during the throw. It is required to have the stationary foot on the sideline while the throw is being performed. The defensive player must be at least 3 meters (10 ft.) away from the thrower. The throw-in may be performed with either one or two hands. A throw-in also occurs when a defensive player (excluding the goalkeeper) is the last to touch the ball causing it to go out of bounds over the goal line, but not into the goal. This type of throw-in is taken on the sideline at the nearest corner where the ball went out of bounds.

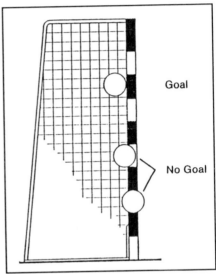

Figure 1.4   Goal Line - Ball out of bounds.

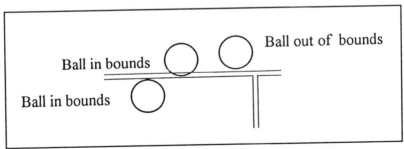

Figure 1.5   Sideline - Ball out of bounds.

THROW-OFF

A ball crossing the goal line outside the goal and last touched or played by the offensive team, or touched by the goalkeeper on a shot at the goal when the goalkeeper was the only defender touching the ball, results in a throw-off by the goalkeeper. This throw must be executed from within the goal area in any manner preferred by the goalkeeper. Defensive players must stay outside the 9 meter line during the throw-off. A goal can be scored directly from a goalkeeper's throw-off.

FOULS

Common fouls are called for such violations as faulty substitution of players, faulty throw-ins, intentional playing across goal line or sideline, body contact or striking an opponent resulting in loss of possession or failure to complete the play. The defender must be between the player and the goal. The foul is not always called if contact was not too hard or if the defender had good defensive position. The penalty for common fouls is a free throw. Free throws are also awarded for double dribbles, taking more than 3 steps, holding the ball more than 3 seconds, offensive player charges, illegal picking, holding, pushing and unnecessary rough play.

Flagrant fouls are called for violations such as taking the ball away from a player; obstruction with arms, hands, or legs; grabbing an opponent; pushing or forcing an opponent into the goal area; and shooting or throwing the ball at an opponent intentionally. In addition to the free throw (or penalty throw) for the opposing team, a caution (yellow card) may be issued by the referee. If the conduct or foul is repeated, the player is suspended for 2 minutes from the game and the team must play short. The third suspension of the same player results in a disqualification from the remainder of the game. The referee will signal this action by holding up a red card.

PENALTIES

A *Free throw* is awarded for all other fouls and infringements of the rules, similar to a violation in basketball. The free throw is taken immediately without the referee handling the ball, from the place the violation occurred. If the foul occurs between the 6 and 9 meter lines, however, the ball is put into play from the 9 meter line closest to the point of the infraction. All offensive players must be outside the 9 meter line and all defensive players must be a least 3 meters from the ball. The thrower must have one foot continuously in contact with the court and must make a throw or pass within 3 seconds. The advantage rule applies to free throws. A goal may be scored directly from the free throw.

A *penalty shot* is awarded when an offensive player is fouled and the referee feels that the player had a good chance to score when they were fouled. This is a free throw (shot) at the opponent's goal from the penalty mark (7 meter line) with only the goalkeeper defending and being at least 3 meters from the thrower until the shot is taken. Any player on the offensive team may take the shot. The player taking the shot must keep one foot in contact with the ground at all times. Once the ball is made ready for play and the referee sounds the whistle, the shooter has 3 seconds to take the shot. All other players must be outside the 9 meter line.

A *Referee's Throw* is a rarely used method to restart play when there is some interruption of the game that was not directly attributable to either team. Some examples are: players of both teams infringed the rules simultaneously, the ball touched the ceiling or any fixed equipment attached above the playing court or the game was interrupted without any infringement of the rules committed and with no team being in possession of the ball. The referee stands in the area where the interruption occurred and throws the ball into the air. All players, with the exception of one from each team, must remain at a distance of at least 3 meters from the referee who is taking the throw. Both players who are jumping for the ball stand next to the referee, each on the side nearest to their own goal. With the toss, the two players may reach and grab the ball or direct it to a teammate, but not until the ball has reached its apex and has started downward. This action is similar to the jump ball used in basketball.

REFEREE

The speed of the game, in addition to the allowable body contact makes good referees extremely important in team handball. When a foul or infraction occurs, the players should look at the referees. The referee points with one hand where the ball should be taken for a free throw. The other hand is used to indicate in what direction the ball will be moving when put back into play by the free throw. The referee does not handle the ball on any foul, infraction, or violation. The player retrieves the ball and puts it into play as quickly as possible. The referee uses hand signals for explanation of the calls and does not talk. A regular game is refereed by two officials. One moves to half-court to cover the outer area of play, while the other referee moves down to the goal line to be in a position to determine if the ball has crossed the goal line for a score. In international play the authority of the referees is absolute.

GOAL AREA

This is the area that extends from the goal line out to the 6 meter line, also referred to as the goal area line. Only the goalkeeper is allowed to enter the goal area. The goal area, which includes the goal area line, is regarded as entered when a player touches it with any part of the body. If an offensive player is in the goal area or on the goal area line, with or without the ball, the ball is awarded to the opponent and any goal that may have been scored is not counted. If the defensive team gains an advantage by being in the goal area, a penalty throw is awarded. A ball inside the goal area belongs to the goalkeeper. However, the ball is not considered to be in the goal area if it is in the air. Any ball that ends up inside the goal area, regardless of how it got there, belongs to the goalie. The goalkeeper is the only player who can put the ball back into play.

2 CHAPTER

BASIC PLAYING SKILLS

This chapter will focus on the basic skills needed to play team handball. Since the team handball player utilizes many of the same skills and techniques used by basketball players, many basketball drills can be used for practice. The skills covered in this chapter are passing, dribbling, shooting, and running (with and without the ball).

BALL HANDLING

HOLDING THE BALL

In handball, the ball should always be held with one hand when dribbling or passing. It is important for the player to be able to hold the ball without looking at it. It should be held comfortably in the hand so that the maximum surface area is covered.

The fingers and the palm are the basic points of contact with the ball. The thumb and little finger are the most important fingers for holding the ball. The other fingers give direction to and control the ball. When holding the ball the thumb and little finger should be spread very widely. The hand should be open but not to the point of being stiff as this will reduce the movement of the wrist. The ends of the fingers should squeeze the ball, making a slight impression in it. All but the very center of the palm of the hand touches the ball. When the ball is held correctly, there is approximately one finger breadth between the ball and the center of the palm. (See figures 2.1-2.4).

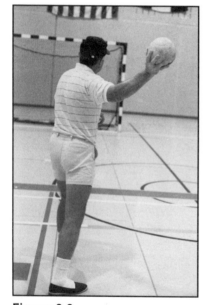

Figure 2.1

Figure 2.2

Figure 2.3

Figure 2.4

RECEPTION OF THE BALL

The ball should be received by the player with the ends of the fingers making contact with the ball and the inside of the palm touching the ball slightly. It should always be received with two hands.

To insure successful reception of the ball certain criteria must be met. The player must be alert to accept a pass at any time. The receiver of the pass should look forward or watch the defense while using peripheral vision to observe the passer. The receiver should glance at the passer only occasionally to avoid allowing the defense to anticipate the pass reception. To protect the ball from the opponent the receiver should place their body between the passer and the defender before the pass is made.

It is very important for the player to feel confident when receiving the ball. They should make visible contact with it just prior to receiving it. To receive the ball the player's arms should extend from the body and then give with the ball as it is received to slow the speed of it. Once the ball is obtained the player must be concerned with holding it securely and maintaining possession of it. The receiver must immediately be prepared for the next move whether it be a shot, dribble or pass.

RECEPTION OF PASSES

The manner in which the player receives the ball is determined by the type of pass thrown (Some examples of this are described in the following).

Frontal Passes

To receive these passes the arms should be extended and stretched toward the ball. The height of the arms will vary according to the placement of the pass. The hands should be open and cupped with the fingers up and thumbs facing each other and almost touching.

Lateral Passes

These passes are received with the same hand and arm movements outlined above with the addition of a new movement which is

---

the turning of the trunk toward the side from which the ball is coming. The ball is received by the arm on the opposite side of the body from which the ball is coming. The arm on the same side as the ball is used to stabilize the ball in the hands.

Ground Passes

a. When the receiver is stationary and the ball is moving, the ball is picked up by the receiver with both hands, palms facing each other.

b. When the receiver is moving and the ball is stationary, the receiver scoops up the ball with the hand of the dominant arm and uses the opposite hand to secure the ball.

c. When the receiver and ball are moving, in opposite directions, the ball is received in the same manner as stated above.

d. When the receiver and ball are moving in the same direction, the receiver scoops up the ball with the hand of the non-dominant arm and uses the hand of the dominant arm to secure the ball.

Handling the Ball

Handling the ball occurs between the time it is received by the player until it is passed or shot by the player. The length of time the ball will be handled is determined by the game situation. Most of the time the player's next move has been decided prior to reception. The player may choose to dribble, pass or shoot.

CONTROL OF THE BALL

There are two methods of taking the ball to a passing or shooting position after the player has received the ball and taken control of it. In the first method, the throwing arm is rotated forward in a downward arc, passing below the player's waist. The arm then continues backward in an arc to the shooting (or passing) position with the arm extended behind the body with the elbow bent slightly. The shoulder on the same side as the throwing arm is back with the opposite shoulder facing the direction of the shot. In the second method, the throwing arm moves the ball directly from the area in front of the body to the shooting position. The arm moves in a rotating motion above the shoulders rather than below the waist.

The first method results in a more powerful and versatile shot and is used when the player has adequate time, distance and little pressure from the defense.

The second method results in a lob shot or a bounce shot and is used when a rapid response is necessary.

PASSING

Passing is the most important skill in team handball. It allows a player to move the ball quickly and accurately and to advance the ball and set up scoring opportunities. Several principles apply to all passes.

1. The type of pass, and the velocity of the pass, is usually determined by the speed of the intended receiver and the distance between the passer and the receiver.
2. While players are learning the fundamentals of passing, the non-throwing hand should point in the direction of the throw. Once the throw has been mastered and the players start to play in competitive games, the players will not want to use this technique because the opponent will know the intended direction of the pass.
3. When throwing and catching the ball, it is recommended that the players use the fingers, rather than the palm of the hand, to insure consistent control of the ball.
4. Proper balance should be maintained and the body weight should be evenly distributed to help insure more accurate passes. During the throwing phase, the body weight should be shifted from the back foot to the front foot maintaining momentum behind the ball for a crisp pass. Off-balance passes should only be thrown in improvised or emergency situations. They usually result in a bad pass and a turnover to the opponent.
5. The correct throwing pattern requires the player to step forward with the leg on the side of the body of the non-throwing hand. For beginning players it is important for them to step in the direction of the throw. For players at

the elite levels this is not as important because they know where the ball is going to be passed. Deception in passing is a very critical strategy.

6. Passing requires a quick flick with either the wrist or elbow rather than extensive wind-up.
7. The type of pass utilized depends on the specific situation which is presented to the player.
8. After making a pass, the player should try to penetrate the defense and look for a return pass.
9. The ball should be thrown to a teammate at chest level so it can be easily handled and put into play.
10. It is important to make a threatening motion (fake) to score before passing to a teammate.
11. Players should make short, crisp and frequent passes.
12. The length of the stride of the lead leg should correspond approximately to the length of the pass.

SET PASS

This pass is initiated with both feet on the floor in an asymmetrical position. The foot of the leg opposite the shooting arm is in front. The upper arm is parallel to the floor with the arm bent at the elbow in a 90 degree angle. The palm is facing the direction of the pass with the fingers pointing upward. The trunk is turned back in the direction of the shooting arm. The throwing shoulder is back.

When the shot is executed, the trunk turns at the hip in the direction of the throw. The shoulders immediately follow and the arm completes the pass with a slight flick of the wrist at the end. This pass can be directed frontally or laterally as the situation warrants. This is the most frequently used pass (See figure 2.5).

Figure 2.5

BOUNCE PASS

This pass is thrown so the ball hits the floor three to four feet in front of the receiving player. Since the ball will lose some of its energy when it strikes the ground, it is important that the receiving player be moving toward the passer. The receiver should catch the ball at the waist level or below. This pass is used when the player is surrounded by defensive players and the ball needs to be advanced inside to another offensive player. The bounce pass can be made with either one or two hands. The two hand pass is done like the chest pass, except the ball is bounced on the floor. In the one hand bounce pass, the offensive player has the advantage of stepping to either side of the defensive player to pass around them (See figure 2.6).

Figure 2.6

CLOSE HAND-OFF PASS

This is a pass that is usually made in very close quarters around the goal area. One player merely hands the ball to a teammate in the manner of handing off a football. Deception is of utmost importance in this pass. This is a pass that should be used by players at higher skill levels. Since the defense is close to the players making this pass, the probability of the pass being intercepted is very high. The hand-off can be done to either the front or back of the player. This pass usually requires practice in very controlled situations (See figure 2.7).

Figure 2.7

HOOK PASS

The hook pass can be utilized by a player who is closely guarded by two or more defensive players. It can also be used when a player is in the air during a jump-shot. The player releases the ball at the top of the jump with a twist of the wrist directing the ball to the desired receiver. This pass is very similar to the hook shot in basketball. In some parts of the world it is called a jump pass (See figure 2.8).

Figure 2.8

JUMP PASS

When normal passing lanes are impeded by the defense, a player can pass by jumping high into the air and throwing the ball to one of the teammates. This pass is usually used in the area of the 6 meter line, since this is where most of the defensive traffic occurs (See figure 2.9).

Figure 2.9

Passes which are normally used for **longer** distances include:

BEHIND THE SHOULDER PASS

This pass is a fake set shot followed by a diagonal pass to a player in position behind the passer. The pass is begun with the arm slightly flexed at shoulder height with the palm of the hand facing the passer's body. The passer's trunk is turned towards the hand holding the ball. The pass starts as a faked forward motion of the arm, or flexion of the elbow, and ends with a flick of the wrist and hand to propel the ball in a backward direction (See figure 2.10).

Figure 2.10

WRIST PASS

This pass is the same as the shoulder pass except the hand rotates, releasing the ball to the side rather than forward. Because of the unusual arm motion, the ball tends to have a twisting, sinking trajectory away from the intended target. This pass is best used by more advanced players (See figure 2.11).

Figure 2.11

BASIC PASSING TECHNIQUES

An accurate throw will usually result in an accurate catch. Some basic techniques of catching a ball include:

1. Whenever possible, players should try to catch the ball with two hands to insure best possible control.
2. The player should always attempt to catch the ball with the finger tips spread apart. Whenever possible, the player should not allow the ball to make contact with the palm of the hand.
3. The elbows should be flexed and the body relaxed to absorb the impact of the incoming ball.
4. Whenever possible, the receiver should move forward to meet the ball, maintaining eye contact with the ball as it comes into his or her hands.
5. Upon receiving a pass, a player should immediately be prepared to shoot, dribble, or pass the ball again.

DRIBBLING

In team handball the dribble is used to advance the ball up the court when a player is not closely guarded and to gain an advantage when attempting to move the ball for purposes of attacking the goal or setting up a possible scoring play. Because of their strong basketball orientation, most American players have a tendency to dribble too much in team handball. It is important to keep the body low for protection and ease of movement and also to keep the ball low. The dribbler's head should be kept up to watch for an open space or possible pass or shot. It needs to be emphasized that good passing can move the ball down the court much faster than a dribble, so all players should look for the pass before taking the dribble. There are two types of dribbles used in team handball which are different than the dribble used in basketball.

SINGLE DRIBBLE (WITH TWO HANDS)

In this type of dribble, the player is permitted to take three steps, bounce the ball before their fourth step touches the ground and catch it. The player is now permitted to take three more steps before having to give up the ball. If the player decides to stop with the ball after catching it from the dribble, he or she may maintain possession of the ball for three seconds before having to pass or shoot. This dribbling rule, combined with the three steps permitted before and after the dribble, make for a much more wide open offensive game. In soccer a typical score may be 2-1 or 1-0 while in team handball game scores of 29-26 are not uncommon. The use of the steps before and after the dribble accounts for much of the scoring. Former basketball players learning the game of team handball find this the most difficult skill to learn. In basketball, once the dribble is picked up the player must exercise his or her options of passing or shooting. It takes many months of practice to add the three allowable steps after picking up the dribble.

CONTINUOUS DRIBBLE

This type of team handball dribble is similar to that used in basketball except that the players may take as many steps as they desire with each dribble. Here the double dribble rule of basketball also applies. That is, the player may not catch the ball off the dribble and then start dribbling again. The continuous dribble is best utilized when the offensive player is in the open court and moving quickly down the court in the attacking line. When the defense closes in the dribble should be abandoned in favor of short crisp passes.

SHOOTING

The primary objective of the game of team handball is to score goals. The only way to score goals is by shooting the ball toward the goal. Shooting will occur in team handball at about the same frequency as in basketball. Players must learn to be patient and work their offensive patterns, trying to create an opportunity to shoot and score a goal. Team handball is an aggressive game and offensive players must continuously press forward toward the opponents goal. Because the defensive team is permitted to make physical contact to thwart the offense, players must utilize physical skills as well as mental toughness to get into positions which allow them good scoring shots. The following are suggested basic principles for the various types of shots used in team handball.

1. The shooter should have a definite shooting direction in mind prior to releasing the ball. Shots that lack power and proper angle or partially blocked shots can be easily handled by the goalkeeper and often result in fastbreak situations for the opposing team. The most vulnerable shooting lanes are the high and low corners of the goal mouth. Shots directed to the lower corners of the goal have greater scoring percentages. Many of the more skilled players will bounce the ball off the floor in these low corners, where there is more room for error on the part of the goalie.

2. The momentum of the shooter should always be in the direction of the goal. There needs to be sufficient power on the shot to get the ball past the goalkeeper.

3. The use of deception is critical. The shooter should attempt to draw the goalkeeper towards one corner of the goal and, depending upon the commitment of the goal-keeper, should direct the shot to the opposite corner.

4. The offensive player should not try to score from extreme angles. The corner offensive players need to be aware of their position on the court so they leave themselves good shooting opportunities.

5. If there is a defensive player directly in front of the shooter, the shooter will have to jump above or to the side of the player to have the opportunity to make a goal. Throwing the ball directly into the defender will not result in a goal.

6. The offensive players should not shoot from beyond 15 meters. These shots are usually handled very easily by the goalkeeper. The most effective shots are taken from between the 6 and 9 meter lines.

7. When the shooter has penetrated the defense and has only the goalie to beat, the shooter must be absolutely certain that the shot for the goal is made from outside the 6 meter line.

TECHNIQUES OF SPECIFIC SHOTS

JUMP SHOT

This is one of the most widely used shots in team handball. The shot primarily involves the use of the shoulder throw (pass) in which the ball is released at the height of the jump with the momentum of the body directed toward the goal rather than falling away. By jumping high into the air, the player is able to see the goal more clearly and can determine the direction of the intended shot (See figure 2.12).

Figure 2.12

DIVE SHOT

This shot also utilizes the shoulder throw (pass). The shooter stretches the body out and directs momentum toward the goal. The ball should be released at the last moment and as close to the goal mouth as possible. The diving motion of the shooter will put the body into a position horizontal to the ground. The ball should be released with a combination of a shoulder and wrist flick. The shock of the fall should be absorbed by putting both arms out in front of the body to act as a cushion. This shot is usually attempted by very skilled players. Many of the floors used for indoor games are very hard, making this shot dangerous (See figure 2.13).

Figure 2.13

UNDERHAND SHOT

This shot utilizes the side arm throwing motion. The shooter turns the body so the torso opposite the throwing arm is toward the goal. The side arm throw that is generated by this twisting action of the upper body results in a very powerful shot. An additional factor that can be used to help generate more power is to utilize a crossover step just before turning the body and releasing the ball. This shot is used when the regular scoring lanes (between the opponent's waist and shoulders) are cut off. This shot is usually completed from a low trajectory with a continuous follow through (See figure 2.14).

Figure 2.14

REVERSE SHOT

This shot is usually used around the 6 meter line (goal area line) when the defender is playing behind or overplaying to the shooter's dominant side. When the player is unable to execute a normal shot because of the defensive pressure, he or she should first lower the center of gravity by bending the knees. The next step should be to make a strong fake to the normal shooting pattern, then turn and quickly pivot away from the regular shooting motion releasing the ball backward toward the goal. Although this type of shot will not be very powerful, the shooter hopes to surprise the goalkeeper and score before the goalie can recover from the initial body fake. As the ball is released body force should be directed toward the goal (See Figure 2.15).

Figure 2.15

SIDE SHOT

This is a relatively weak shot but the proper element of surprise can make it successful. It is most frequently used close to the goal area when an attempted shot with a regular shoulder throw is prevented by a defender. The shooter, starting with the back to the opponent's goal, should drop the shoulder on the non shooting side of the body, then step back across the body with the foot on the shooting side. This will put the body in a position to allow the shooter to release the ball forward into the goal (See Figure 2.16).

Figure 2.16

LOB SHOT

This shot is often used in a 1-on-1 fast break situation and also in certain 2-on-1 situations. When the goalkeeper comes out of the goal to challenge the potential shot, the offensive player merely lobs the ball over the goalie's head into the goal or to their teammate if this is a 2-on-1 situation. Timing is of the utmost importance in the execution of this shot (See figure 2.17).

Figure 2.17

PENALTY SHOT

This shot is unique in that it can only be taken as the result of a serious violation of the rules. The opportunity to take this shot has be awarded by the referees. Any player on the offended team may take the penalty shot. This shot is taken from the 7 meter penalty mark. It is a 1-on-1 situation with the goalie as the only defender. The goalkeeper may move about and come within three meters of the penalty line. The player who is awarded the penalty shot cannot move his or her feet or touch the penalty line until after the ball has been released. The player has three seconds in which to shoot from the time the referee blows the whistle to commence the execution of the penalty throw. The type of shot normally used in this situation is the shoulder or side arm throw. All other players must remain outside the 9 meter line until the shot is taken. They should strategically position themselves around the goal to be ready for a blocked shot by the goalkeeper or a direct rebound off the goal posts (See figure 2.18).

Figure 2.18

BASIC PLAYING STRATEGIES

This chapter will focus on the basic strategy for both the offensive and defensive teams. The narrative information will be supplemented by a number of diagrams, patterns, and photographs showing how these basic strategies can be incorporated into the game of team handball. It is hoped that this chapter will appeal to the most advanced player, as well as to the novice just being introduced to this exciting game.

BASIC POSITION

In the game of handball it is critical for the player to be thinking one or two seconds ahead of the action of the game. Due to the speed of the game, the player must constantly be alert and ready to react as quickly as possible. He or she must be able to anticipate, prior to receiving the ball, what the next move will be. The basic position is extremely important as it prepares the player to make that next movement as effectively and efficiently as possible.

When assuming the basic position, the player's body should be balanced in a natural, comfortable and effective position. The head is up in a normal position to improve peripheral vision, the trunk is bent forward slightly and the legs are bent slightly with one in front of the other. Usually, the leg opposite the shooting arm is in front to enable the player to move forward quickly when necessary. The feet are flat on the floor with the player's weight distributed equally across the soles. The arms are semi-flexed, with the hands ready to receive the ball. The basic position is the same for all players except that the second line player's (wings and circles) body is in a slightly lower position than the first line player's (backcourt players).

BASIC OFFENSIVE STRATEGY

A team is in the offensive or attacking mode when it is in possession of the ball or about to be in possession of the ball. The three basic offensive player positions in team handball are the wing players, the circle runner and the back court players. Even though many of the positions may be interchangeable during any given offensive attack, each of the positions has certain responsibilities that should be carried out by the specific player in that position.

PLAYERS

WING PLAYERS

The wing players (usually two) must be quick, agile and able to lead the fast break attack. These players attack the goal when shooting and should be able to protect the ball against the defense. These players are also excellent ball handlers and dribblers and should be able to see the entire field of play ahead of them. These players usually take shots from deep in the attacking zone. These shots need to be taken from a low angle from the side of the goal. A strong, diving sidearm shooter is desired here.

CIRCLE RUNNER

The circle runner is usually the biggest, tallest, and strongest player on the court. This player is generally a blocker, setting screens for the wing players and backcourt players. The circle runner needs strength to handle the ball in heavy traffic and coordinates moves with the other offensive players. Like the basketball center, this player operates much of the time with his or her back to the attacking goal. This player will usually utilize a spin shot to try and divide the defense and attempt to score. Deceptive fakes are also utilized by the circle runner to get the defense to commit before dropping the ball off to an open player for a clear shot at the goal.

BACK COURT PLAYERS

The back court players (usually three) should be strong, hard throwers who can pass, run, dribble and shoot well. These players should be the best all-around athletes on the court and should provide most of the team scoring. Most teams will employ the three basic phases of offensive attack which are the fastbreak, the secondary fastbreak, and the patterned, organized phases. *Basic offensive positions* (See figure 3.1).

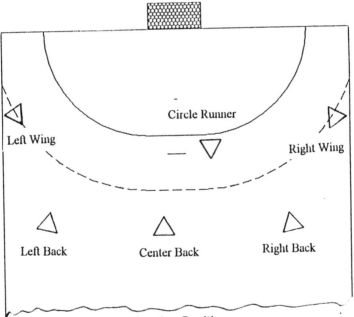

Figure 3.1 Basic Offensive Positions

FASTBREAK

When a team gets possession of the ball by means of a blocked shot, violation or an interception (turn-over), the team is in the position to begin the fastbreak. The fastbreak has the same basic characteristics as those used in basketball. It involves great speed, a few accurate passes, and outmaneuvering the short-handed defense. The goal-keeper can contribute to starting the fastbreak by stopping shots in the manner that will allow them to recover the ball quickly, initiating the breakaway pass to breaking teammates. The wings generally are among the players in the first wave. They tend to stay wide as they move to their offensive positions at the other end of the court. The other backcourt players normally follow in the second wave and, in lieu of a quick goal, bring the ball up court with minimal use of dribbling (See figure 3.2).

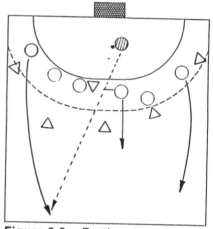

Figure 3.2   Fastbreak

SECONDARY FASTBREAK

When the fastbreak does not end in a score or the first wave of the fastbreak is covered, it is followed by a second wave of attack. This secondary break is executed by the players who are trailing the initial fastbreak attempt. This phase of the offense is based upon catching the defenders before they get organized into their usual defensive positions.

ORGANIZED PATTERNED PHASE

If the first two phases of attack do not result in a goal, the team goes into its patient, systematic attack. This offensive strategy can be stationary or moving. The moving offense can be a patterned or free lance style of play. Those familiar with basketball offenses will recognize the many variations of screens, picks, as well as give and go in the team handball offense. Offensively, players should focus on total team movement, remain spread out, think pass before dribble, move the ball quickly and always pose a scoring threat.

THE 3-3 ATTACK

The 3-3 attack is the basic offense in team handball. The first line of attack is the backcourt players. The wings and circle runner make up the second line of attack. Figures 3.3 - 3.7 are some examples of 3-3 attack system.

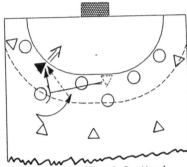

Figure 3.3   The 3-3 attack

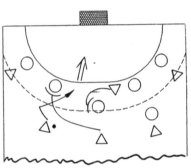

Figure 3.4

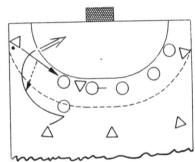

Figure 3.5

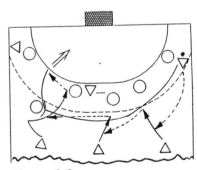

Figure 3.6

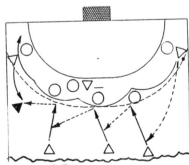

Figure 3.7

THE 2-4 ATTACK

Another type of offensive system is the 2-4 attack. The first line consists of two backcourt players. The second line includes two circle runners and the two wings (See figure 3.8).

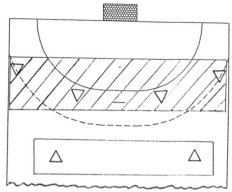

Figure 3.8   The 2-4 attack

Movement in the 2-4 attack must include good coordination between the circle runners, backcourts and wings. For example, the circle runner can set a pick for the left wing. The wing attacks to the right and receives the pass from the left backcourt (See figure 3.9).

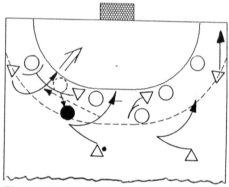

Figure 3.9

DEFENSIVE STRATEGY

Good defensive play allows the team to attack with confidence. The team works together as a unit in team handball defense. The first responsibility of the defending team is stopping the fastbreak then organizing into their defense system. The defensive attack must be carried out suddenly to prevent the offensive attackers from anticipating the defensive strategy.

RESPONSIBILITIES OF THE DEFENSIVE PLAYERS

The attitude of the defensive player should be similar to that of the goalkeeper defending the goal. The defender must maintain maximum attention or alertness to control the movements of attackers. The defender should aggressively respond to an offensive attack and attempt to dominate the offense using a wide range of technical resources. When guarding against an attacker 1 on 1, the defender should use adequate movements to keep the opponent at bay. In addition, the defender must always keep the ball, as well as potential attackers in sight.

Marking refers to the act of identifying a potential attacker and observing the actions of the attacker to ready oneself to guard against that player's attack. The defender must be ready at any time as the situation warrants, to leave one player and begin actively guarding another player whom he or she has been marking. While the defender is guarding this player he or she begins marking any other player that presents as a potential attacker. Marking will be covered in greater detail in Chapter 4.

SPECIFIC TYPES OF DEFENSIVE STRATEGIES

The 6-0 defense is the most common defensive system. The 6-0 defense means that the starting position of each player is next to the 6 meter line (See figure 3.10).

The 6-0 defense is a combination of a zone and player to player defense. Each player has an individual re-

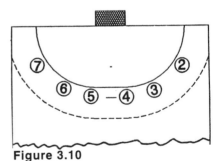

Figure 3.10

sponsibility in addition to helping their teammates. Players should count the opponents to determine which opponent is their responsibility. The first defenders, the wings, guard the first player in the offensive attack on their side of the court. The second defender on each side guards the second offensive player. The middle defenders must decide between themselves who will guard the circle runner and who will be on the backcourt. The movement of the circle runner will change their responsibility so communication is essential to insure that everyone is being defended. *Counting the opponent in the 6-0 defense* (See figure 3.11).

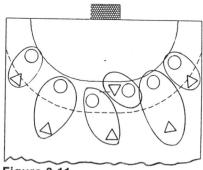

Figure 3.11

If any offensive player changes position, the defense follows them only until they can give them to the next defender. For example if the attacking wing (B) decides to run toward the center, the wing defender follows the player until the second defender (2) can take the attacking wing (B). The wing defender's responsibility is now the backcourt player (A) the first attacking player on his or her side. *Offensive player changes position* (See figure 3.12).

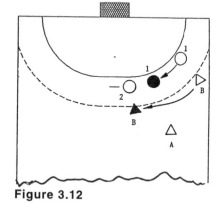

Figure 3.12

If the wing continues toward the other side of the court, the same process of passing the wing to the next defender would continue. *Player 2 has Player A. Player 3 passes Player B to Player 4 and shifts to cover Player C* (See figure 3.13).

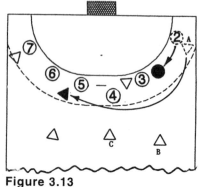

Figure 3.13

In addition to counting the attacking players, the defense forms a triangle in front of each attacking player with the ball. The player directly opposite the attacking player meets them at the 9 meter line. Their teammates shift and help cover to the right and left of the ball, forming a "wall" in front of the attacking opponent. *Forming a defensive triangle in front of the left backcourt* (See figure 3.14). *Defense shifts to form a triangle in front of center backcourt* (See figure 3.15).

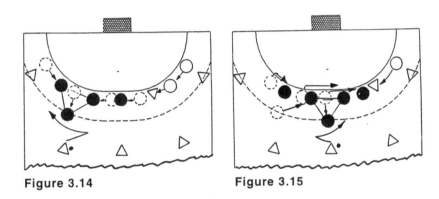

Figure 3.14   **Figure 3.15**

Defense shifts to form a triangle in front of right backcourt (See figure 3.16).

Players go out to the 9 meter line to meet the attacking player then shift diagonally with the ball to help their teammates and to cover the 6 meter line. *Defending the ball then shifting to help a teammate defend the pass* (See figure 3.17).

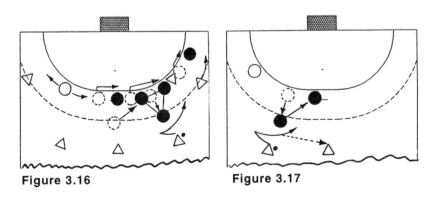

Figure 3.16   **Figure 3.17**

Players must shift with the ball to help teammates and at the same time count the opponents to determine their individual responsibility.

The wings shift with every pass made to help form the wall. However, because of the extreme angle of the wing shot, the wing does not leave the 6 meter line unless defending a back-court player. The attacking wing is forced to beat the defender at the 6 meter line. The wings defend by laterally moving along the 6 meter line. *Defensive movement of the wings* (See figure 3.18).

Good individual defense is dependent on quick movement of the legs to position one's body in front of the attacking player. Strength is important after the defense has gained the proper position to prevent the opponent from scoring.

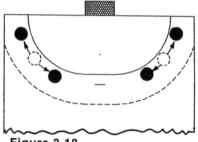

Figure 3.18

GOALIE

The goalie is probably the most important player on the court. The main purpose of the goalie is to block shots of the opponents. The initiation of the fastbreak after a save is another important role for the goalie.

The goalie moves in the goal area in relation to the position of the ball and to the offensive players on the court. Quick reflexes, coolness on the court, courage, and size contribute greatly to the goalie's success. The ideal weight for the goalie is 195 to 198 pounds; the ideal height is 6' 3" to 6' 5".

The ready position allows the goalie to move in any direction. Standing up allows the goalie to fill the cage as much as possible and cover more area, unlike a basketball defensive ready position. Arms should be held in a comfortable raised position able to move up and down and sideways (See figures 3.19, 3.20, 3.21 and 3.22).

Figure 3.19

Figure 3.20

Figure 3.21

Figure 3.22

DEFENSIVE STRATEGIES

INTRODUCTION

In team handball, defensive players are each assigned a specific task, as well as being expected to function as part of the unit in a zone defense.

Defensive positioning is determined by the effective area of play and positioning of the offensive attacker and ball. Defensive strategy is chosen in response to the type of offensive strategy used in attack.

AREA OF PLAY

The area of play is determined by the capabilities of the players. The effective shot is normally no longer than 12m. It is very difficult to execute it within a 10 degree angle between the goal post and the side line. Consequently, the effective area of play, or the area that must be defended, is between the 6 and 12 m lines and between the line of the 10º angle on the left side of the goal to the same line on the right side.

To best defend this area, the players should be positioned in the area between the line of the 40º angle with the side line and the

perpendicular; be prepared to cover the area up to the line of the 20°
angle in response to movement of the ball (See figure 4.1).

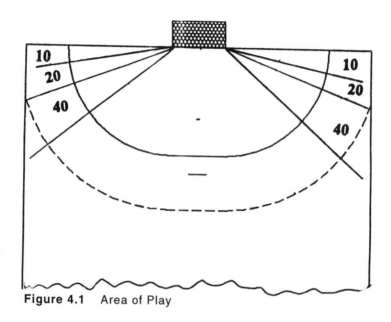

Figure 4.1 Area of Play

RELATIONS BETWEEN PLAYER, BALL AND TYPE OF DEFENSE

There are two fundamental principles of defense: 1) Only one
player can ultimately score; 2) A goal can be scored only with the ball.
When basing defensive strategy on the first principle, the players
concentrate the majority of their attention on the opponent (man-to-
man defense) and the remainder on the ball. The attackers determine
the movements and concentration of the defensive system.

When strategy is based on the second principle, the majority
of the defensive attention is on the ball and it is the ball that determines
the movement and concentration of the defense. The most effective
defense is one which combines both principles in their defensive
strategy and maintains depth, density and width.

DEFENSIVE PLAY

The defender must be aggressive and act decisively, never hesitating and never giving the offense the idea that they can overcome the defense. In team handball, there are two lines of defense: court players are the first line; the goalie, the second. The first line defense must protect the goal by preventing or weakening the offensive attack. They work as a unit, moving laterally and forward, to maintain a defense that is deep, dense and wide.

The defender must be able to anticipate the attacker's next move and deny the possibility of gaining an advantage or creating an overload on the defense. The defensive objective must be to meet the offense on the 9 meter line and prevent them from receiving the ball or advancing further toward the goal. If the offense goes beyond the 9 meter line the defense must respond with 110% enthusiasm to disrupt the offensive play. When the offensive player is in mid court, the defender should concentrate on denying the player the pass; if the player is a wing, the defender should concentrate on forcing the player to the back corners of the court to prevent them from having an easy shot should they gain access to the ball.

To be an effective defender, the player must always have the ball and an opponent in sight. The defender must be able to anticipate where the ball will travel and what the player may do next. In team handball it is said that each player defends one and one-half players, meaning they actively defend against one attacker while marking, or observing, another who poses a potential threat. The game situation can change rapidly such that potential attacker becomes an actual threat to the goal in a matter of seconds.

MARKING

Marking is an integral part of defensive strategy. For the purpose of discussion, defensive marking can be separated into two types based on the positioning of the players: distance marking and proximity marking. Distance marking, as the name suggests, refers to marking the attacker who is not in the defender's immediate defensive area. In distance marking, the defender achieves control by watching the attackers' movements through intermittent visual contacts. While marking, the defender maintains placement between the attacker and the goal at all times and assumes the basic position facing the opponent. The defender uses smoother, sliding movements to follow the attacker's movements, moving laterally and then forward as the situation warrants.

When the attacker is posing an immediate threat, the defender makes use of proximity marking to control the opponent's dangerous progression toward the goal and deny them possession of the ball. In this case, the defender maintains visual contact with the opponent, trying to anticipate and prevent the player's next move. The defender tries to achieve a position between the attacker and goal, standing slightly more toward the attacker's dominant side. The defender assumes the basic position with the leg on the opponent's dominant side slightly forward, remaining alert and ready to react spontaneously. The defender should move with short and quick sliding movements without crossing the legs to maintain an effective proximity to the player. As the attacker becomes more of an immediate threat the defender works to move closer to the attacker. The defender uses one arm with hand and fingers extended to actively block the ball. The trunk and opposite arm are used to restrict the attacker's movement. The defender's actions should provide just enough resistance to keep the opponent at bay, denying the attacker an offensive advantage.

POSITIONING

Defensive positioning is chosen in response to the attackers' positioning and their role in the offensive attack. The defender must establish a location which allows them to intercept or prevent the pass to the opponent while restricting the opponent's movement. The defender's position should force the opponent to go out of their way to receive a pass, causing the offense to change their plan of attack. The defender's positioning should allow them to react quickly to sudden changes of the attacker's shooting arm. Some specific examples of defensive positioning are as follows:

1. Positioning to block or intercept a pass:

a. **When the defender is between attacker and goal:** In this situation, the defender should establish positioning on the side of the opponent closest to the ball with the leg on the

---

side of the ball forward to prevent movement of the attacker toward the ball. The arm on the side of the ball is used to block the shot while the opposite arm is on the opponent's hip to control the attacker's movement toward that side.

When the player is directly in front of the goal on the 6 meter line, it is advisable to stand in back of the attacker, maintaining trunk-to-trunk contact. The defender should maintain a wide base of support with weight distributed equally on both feet to allow for a quick shift of direction to react to the attacker's position change. The arm on the side of the ball should be extended in front of the player with hand and fingers extended to prevent pass reception, while the opposed hand is on the player's hip to prevent movement in that direction.

b. **When the attacker is between the goal and a defender on the 6 meter line:** In this situation, the defender should place their body on the side of the attacker's shooting arm to deny access to the ball. One arm should be in contact with the attacker's abdomen to monitor their movement and the other arm should be extended to block or intercept the pass. The defender should move back to lock the attacker between himself and the 6 meter line restricting movement and pass reception.

2. Positioning to prevent the attacker from making a shot:

a. **Attacker in set shot facing the defender:** In this situation the defender should place the body between the opponent and goal with a slight inclination toward the side of the shooting arm. The leg on the side of the shooting arm should be forward. The arm on the same side should be extended toward the attacker's shooting arm with hand and fingers extended to prevent the shooter from being able to initiate the shooting motion. The other arm should be making contact with the shooter's hip to prevent movement in that direction.

b. **Attacker in contact with floor and back to defender:** Again, the defender should place themselves between the opponent and goal, but this time, with a slight inclination toward the opposite side of the shooting arm ready to prevent the attacker from pivoting around to the goal to make the shot. The legs should be in a symmetrical position. The arms should be attacking the ball enthusiastically while controlling lateral movement of the attacker. Trunk-to-trunk contact is maintained to help control the attacker's movement.

c. **Attacker in jump shot:** The defender is between the attacker and goal maintaining trunk-to-trunk contact jumping along with the shooter. The defender should jump immediately after the shooter to avoid allowing the shooter to change their shot after the defender has already committed. The arms are extended toward the shooting arm with fingers open wide, attempting to bring the shooting arm down to prevent initiation of the shot.

3. Positioning to block a shot:

a. **Attacker in set shot facing the defender:** In this situation the defender's trunk should be between the shoulder of the shooting arm and the goal. The defender's trunk follows the movement of the shooter. The arms are extended at the moment of the shot with fingers open wide to block the ball. The leg on the same side as the shooting arm is slightly forward and the heel of the back leg is raised to lessen the distance to the shooting arm. In very low shots the defender should block the ball with only one hand to maintain better balance.

b. **Attacker in jump shot:** The defender jumps with the shooter, not before, keeping his or her trunk in line with the shooters: arms are extended with hands and fingers extended to attack the ball. When the shooter is on the 6-meter line and the defender is on the same side as the shooting arm, the defender should attack the ball with only one hand. When on the opposite side as his or her shooting arm, the defender should attack the ball with both hands.

DEFENSE 5-1

This system of Defense 5-1 consists of five defenders near the 6m line and one forward. The forward defender (7) covers an area approximately 3-4m wide between 7m and 10m in the middle of the defensive block. They move in relation to the ball going from 7-10m depending where the attack originates. When the ball is far from this zone, the forward defender moves no farther than 7m. Physically, this player does not have to be tall, but must be agile and aggressive (See figure 4.2).

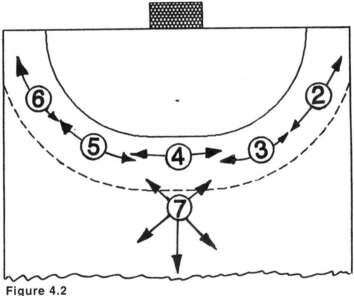

Figure 4.2

The defensive tasks of the forward defender are to prevent shots or passes to the circle, to intercept the ball, bother offensive actions, stop penetrations and block shots. If the offense plays with two circles, the forward must move back toward the 7m line, when there is no pressure in their zone, trying to stop passes and assist the other defenders. If the center or the wing in attacking with the ball penetrates into their area, the forward must react immediately to stop the action.

The five remaining defenders normally work in the area between 6m and 7m. It is advantageous to have tall defenders, especially in positions 3,4, and 5, in order to impair the attacker's view of the goal (See figure 4.2). These five players move laterally as a wall, especially when the ball is near. They move and at all times face the direction of the ball. They move at most one step toward the attacker and do not attack the player with the ball outside the 9m line. Their concentration is focused on blocking the ball, preventing passes to the circle and stopping penetrations. The farther their opponents are from the ball, the farther they will be from those opponents.

The primary objective of the defenders is to cover all the possible passes to the circles, while maintaining continuous visual and physical control of them. Although no specific defender is assigned to cover the circles, it is understood that the players closest to the circle(s) are responsible for their defense (See figure 4.3).

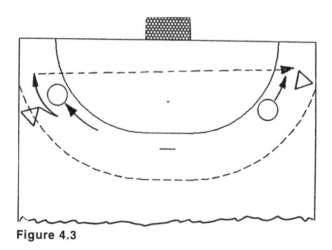

Figure 4.3

The 5-1 zone defense does not have much depth, except in the middle. It is very passive and easily penetrated by good teams. For this reason, this system is used against teams that do not have good shooters or teams whose attack does not have much variation and relies heavily on plays with the circle runner.

This system of defense can be done in combination with a 3-2-1 system to make it stronger. In this case, the forward defender moves back and forth in the center area between 8m and 12m to stop the offensive attack. It can be used as a surprise or as a strategy against teams with fixed combinations.

DEFENSE 3-2-1

In defense 3-2-1, three defenders are near the 6m line, two a little more forward between 7-8m and one more forward between 9-10m. The three defenders on the 6m line (2,3,4) make lateral moves along the 6m line in order to bother the opponents. The next two defenders (5, 6) generally make forward movements forcing the opponent to shoot from far away while reinforcing the defense around the 9m line. The forward (7) controls the court with lateral and forward movements to stop the long shots and passes to players located around the 6m line (See figure 4.4).

Defense 3-2-1 has depth, density and width. It combines the depth of 3-3 with the width of 5-1. The team defending in 3-2-1 should be prepared to move quickly and stop shots from the circle and wing. This system can be effective when used against teams that employ tactical changes to surprise the defense and teams that have both effective long distance shooters and actively scoring circle runners.

4 = left exterior
3 = central
2 = right exterior
6 = left lateral
5 = right lateral
7 = forward

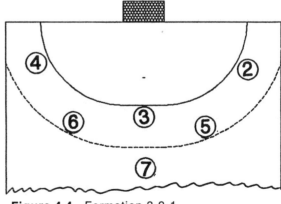

Figure 4.4 Formation 3-2-1

Characteristics of Defenders

The central and both exteriors must have lateral mobility and good sense of the opponent's behavior. They should be able to get the ball away from the opponent inside their area and cover the shots from outside the line. The laterals must have forward and backward mobility, short sprint speed to thwart the opponent's penetration of the defense, quick speed reaction to counteract fakes and the ability to intercept and block passes. The forward must have good forward and lateral mobility, short sprint speed, be effective at intercepting and blocking passes and be able to anticipate fakes.

Advantages

1. It provides stability against the mobility of the attack.
2. It has depth, density, and width. With the exception of the wings and circle, the attacker with the ball is always covered by two defenders for blockage of long shots and passes to the circle.
3. Each player in the system has a specific task to accomplish.
4. The position of the defenders on the court facilitates the execution of the fastbreak. It puts the defenders in a position of advantage over the opponent, especially when the players are able to react and move quickly . The Yugoslavian fastbreak (where the defender who is beaten by the shooter in an attack is part of the first wave of a fastbreak) can work well with Defense 3-2-1.
5. All the players in the system can quickly see when the team recovers the ball from the opponent.

Disadvantages

1. It requires excellent physical conditioning of the players since they must make many short, fast movements to maintain the depth, density and width of the defense.
2. It is difficult to defend in the wing and circle positions.
3. Very few teams have been able to master this system of defense due to the intense physical demands.

Basic Formations and Movements

1. Ball In Center Backcourt (See figure 4.5).

The forward defender is ready for the block and does not allow the player with the ball to penetrate.

Laterals 5 and 6 are located between 6m and 9m, ready to stop the penetration of the player CB if they can get through 7. They also try to intercept the passes to the circle runner.

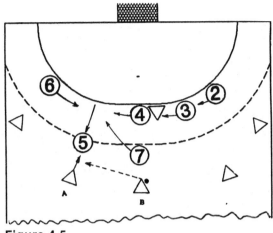

Figure 4.5

The central guards the circle runner all the way into the area between both exteriors since the position of the lateral is not dangerous to the penetration of a second circle runner.

The exteriors are located near the wings to intercept the shots from that position. They guard the circle runners when they pass the position of the laterals and near the wing position to allow the central to keep a position in the middle.

2. Ball in the Left Backcourt (See figure 4.6).

The right lateral (6) is located at 9m ready to block and stop the penetration of A who has the ball.

The center (3) is in the area between the right exterior (4) and the circle runner (E), defending that area against the circle runner. When the circle runner is not near, the center shifts with the ball and lets the circle be guarded by the left lateral (5).

The left lateral (5) is on the 6m line, positioned in front of the left post of the goal. The mission of this defender is to stop the circle runner(s). This places two players (3 and 5) in charge of the circle runners.

The right exterior (4) guards the left wing in offense.

With the ball in the offensive right backcourt, the defensive strategy will be the same, but involving opposite players.)

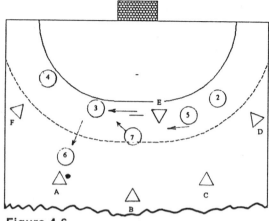

Figure 4.6

3. **Ball in the Wing**
(See figure 4.7).

The exterior (4) guarding the wing with the ball acts very aggressively. The exterior (2) on the opposite side stops the possible pass to the other wing.

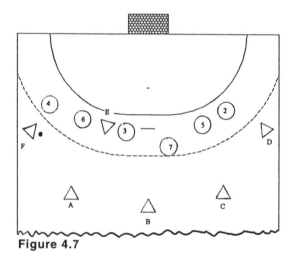

Figure 4.7

The forward defender (7) tries to intercept the pass and the other defenders cover the 6m line against any possible penetration.

In this formation the circle is always between two defenders.

DEFENSE 5 + 1

Defense 5+1 is a collective defense combining both zone and man-to-man defensive strategies. One player is a specialist who guards one attacker man-to-man, usually the opponent's best shooter. Essential qualities of the specialist are speed, wide arm span and the ability to anticipate the movement of the game. The remaining five defenders move near the 6m line as in Defense 6-0. They each cover an area tangent to the next defender and collaborate with the defenders on each side to prevent penetration by the opponent. The defenders are each responsible for an attacker as well as their zone (See figure 4.8).

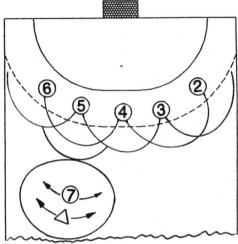

Figure 4.8

In this system the defenders follow all the principles of a good defense in addition to:

1. Accompanying and delivering the attacker only in front of the adjacent defender and only to a defender who is not guarding an opponent with the ball (See figure 4.9).

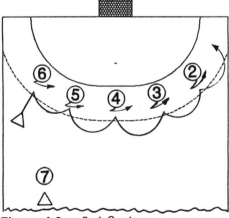

Figure 4.9   5+1 System

---

2. Following the player with the ball (See figure 4.10).

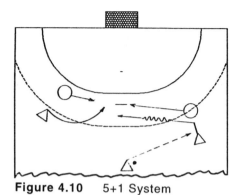

Figure 4.10   5+1 System

3. Communicating and collaborating with the next defender (See figure 4.11).

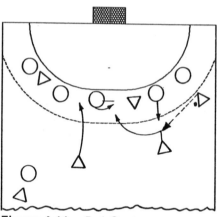

Figure 4.11   5+1 System

4. Switching opponents as the action of the game changes (See figure 4.12.

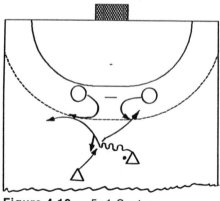

Figure 4.12   5+1 System

5. Stopping the penetration of the attacker with the ball (See figure 4.13).

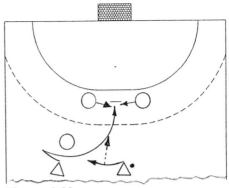

Figure 4.13

6. Guarding the circle runner aggressively to restrict movement and deny pass reception. This enables the defender who is guarding the ball to focus attention on the opponent with the ball without distraction (See figure 4.14).

Figure 4.14

7. The specialist guards the best shooter or the playmaker, close or at a distance. If the attacker goes to the circle, the specialist takes another attacker (See figure 4.15).

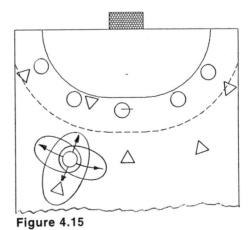

Figure 4.15

8. If there is a pick and roll by the circle runner the specialist needs the help of the defender in charge of the circle runner (See figure 4.16).

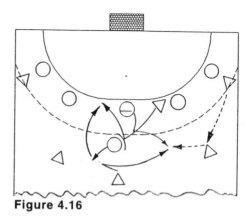

Figure 4.16

9. When an attacker breaks the man-to-man defense he or she must be guarded by the defender closest to the penetration. As soon as the attacker abandons the zone defense, the defender who was guarding this player goes back to the defensive line at the same place and returns to his or her original place when the attack is over.

10. The defender in front of the ball must be helped by the two closest defenders.

This system may be varied as follows:
1. If there are three tall defenders, they can play in the middle while the specialist plays at the 9m line.
2. If there are no tall defenders, four of the defenders can play near 7-8m and leave one defender in charge of the circle runner.
3. It can be played as a classic 5-1 defensive system with the specialist playing the ball and hindering passes in the middle.

This combined system of defense used in 5+1 is very effective. The zone creates problems for the attack while the endurance and special qualifications of the defenders are tapped in one-on-one situations. This system can also aid the less experienced goalie by forcing the offense to make difficult long distance shots.

DEFENSE 4-2

Defense 4-2 utilizes two defensive lines which act as one unit. The first line consists of four players near the 6m line; the second line consists of two advance players around the 9m line. On the first line the two exteriors (2 and 5) play at the 6m line while the two centers (3 and 4) play 1 meter in front of the 6m line. The centers and advance players act together as a tactic parallelogram. To achieve this the advance players form two defensive points that move laterally according to the direction of the ball. The centers shift accordingly to maintain the parallelogram and prevent holes in the defensive block (See figure 4.17, 4.18 and 4.19).

This system is a very open defense, but is also very wide and deep. Each player in the defense is responsible for covering a zone and works as a block to attackers approaching the

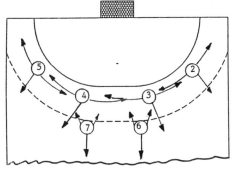

Figure 4.17   System 4-2

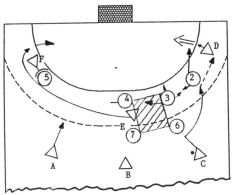

Figure 4.18   Defense 4-2

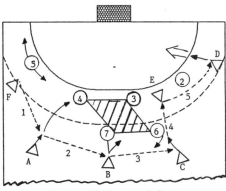

Figure 4.19   Defense 4-2

zone. It is important for the advance players to act decisively and react quickly and for the centers to be able to anticipate and respond to changes in the movement of the game.

To make the system function most effectively the advance players must apply these defensive principles:

1. Bother the play of the attacker, especially their first line. Slow the attackers so they do not get through to the first defensive line.
2. Shift with the ball laterally and move backward toward the ball, trying to stop the pass to the second line in attack.
3. While attacking the opponent with the ball, cover holes and guard the opponent without passing the 9m line.
4. Begin the defensive action with an energetic step forward and arms prepared for defense.
5. Cover the attacker's shooting arm and defensive fakes.
6. Provoke the shooter to shoot from far out.
7. When the attacker passes the ball, return to the first line in the direction of the ball. (This closes the defensive line, making it difficult to penetrate.)
8. Be prepared for the fastbreak when the ball is intercepted by the first line.

Similarly, the total defense must apply the following principles:

1. In addition to the open defense, everybody is part of a closed defensive block that must be maintained.
2. Everyone moves in the direction of the ball.
3. Everyone talks to each other to maintain a collaborative defensive effort.
4. Everyone must remain alert for a change of opponents. During the change of opponents, the defenders work in couples.
5. When an opponent in the first line of attack is guarded directly, the circle must be guarded man-to-man.
6. Work the attacker with the ball until they pass it. Then return to the "block".
7. If an attacker gets past one of the advance players, one of the first line defenders will be in charge of stopping them.
8. Intercept passes through the defensive block and respond with a fastbreak.

Advantages of 4-2:

1. It can be used very effectively against teams with two good back court shooters.
2. It is also effectively used when the goalie is weak in blocking long shots.
3. It presents a strong, closed defense against attacks in the middle of the court.
4. The depth and width of the defense inhibit the clear vision of the attack.
5. It is easy to execute when all players understand their own tasks and play according to the guidelines.

Disadvantages of 4-2

1. The position of the advance players around the 9m line can create the opportunity for picks or pick and rolls by the circle runners.
2. If an advance player is beaten by an attacker, the first line must stop the attacker with man-to-man defense.
3. Big spaces are left in the wings when the exteriors shift to the middle to make the defense more compact. The attacker can take this opportunity to penetrate and shoot. It becomes especially dangerous when the opposing team has strong wing players.

DEFENSE 6-0

In this system, each defender is responsible for a zone in the area between the 9m and 6m lines and guards any attacker who plays in that zone. This system creates a block that works as a unit against all the actions of the opposing team. The defense is set according to the position of the attack and shifts with the direction of the ball, each defender always guarding an attacker (See figure 4.20).

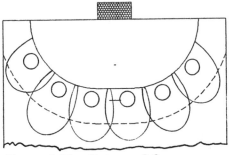

Figure 4.20   Defense 6-0

The defender does not follow the attacker when the attacker switches position, but rather switches opponents. Switching opponents involves reception of the opponent, accompanying the opponent to the next defender and delivery of the opponent to that defender. Only on very rare occasions when there is no defender to switch to, will a defender have to follow an attacker to a different defensive zone. In this system, there are two groups of defenders: the exteriors and the centers. The exteriors (2 and 7) have the responsibility to prevent penetration by the opposing wings and limit their possibilities. They work to prevent shots from their zones (See figure 4.21).

The exteriors move almost exclusively near the 6m line. When the ball is on the opposite side of the court, they shift toward the middle to reinforce that zone. If the attack is in their zone, the defenders must place themselves in the area of possible angles of shots to

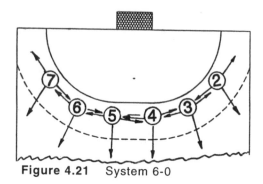

Figure 4.21   System 6-0

limit the attacker's actions. They focus on getting the ball from the attacker, preventing passes and shots at the goal and forming a wall with adjacent defenders to control the attacker and force him or her out of the free throw area. If unable to prevent the shot, they attempt to cover the most favorable angles to make the shot more difficult. If the attacker finally gets the position and jumps inside the circle, the defender must make a final attempt to also jump inside and remove the ball from the attacker's hands.

The exteriors are relied upon to prevent penetration by the attackers behind the defensive block. They must use body positioning and leg work to stop the penetration and force attackers to move out in front of the defenders. This then facilitates the switching of opponents.

The centers (3,4,5,6) are responsible for actions against opponents who are far away and the circle runner. When guarding opponents who do not have the ball the defender will stay near the circle. As soon as the ball gets close to the opponent's zone, the defender must focus on stopping the penetration, attacking the shooting arm, making the pass difficult and avoiding fakes. When the attacker passes the ball, the defender will return to the original position, shifting in the direction of the ball.

When responsible for covering the circle runner, the centers must be ready to utilize aggressive man-to-man defense and collaborate with adjacent defenders in the switching of opponents. The defenders must locate themselves between the ball and the circle runner and between the circle runner and the goal. The defenders in charge of the circle runner are also responsible for blocking shots, collaborating with the goalie and retrieving the rebound balls in the circle area.

When an attacker attempts a 9m throw, the defenders' main objective is to block the ball. To do this the defenders will form a wall with adjacent defenders in the line of the ball. The number of defenders involved will depend on the position of the shooter in relationship to the goal (See figure 4.22). In some instances the defenders will need to collaborate with the goalie, particularly when the shot is originating from the middle of the court. Once the offense executes the play, the defenders return to their original places. At the same time they are studying the positions of the offensive players to avoid the possibility of offensive overload.

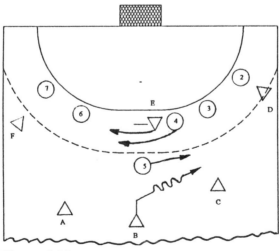

Figure 4.22

Thus the principles of defense that are essential for a successful 6-0 defense are:

1.   Individual coverage of the opponent.
2.   Switching of the opponent.
3.   Shifting with the ball.
4.   Preventing overload by the attackers.
5.   Group blockage.
6.   Preventing screens.
7.   Collaboration with the goalie.
8.   Ongoing communication and collaboration with adjacent defenders.

Most frequent errors in defense 6-0

1.   The defender does not shift; they stay in front of their opponent.
2.   The defender allows the attacker to move easily.
3.   The defender leaves the zone and is beaten one-on-one by the attacker.
4.   The defender allows penetration and does not tell the next defender.
5.   The defender switches an opponent and does not take the next one.
6.   Two defenders guard one attacker.
7.   Nobody guards the attacker with the ball.
8.   The defender reacts too late.
9.   The defender does not return to the circle after going out in 9m.
10. The defender allows the opponent an advantageous position.
11. Two defenders are with the circle runner.
12. One defender decides too late to guard an opponent and disrupts the switching of opponents.
13. The defender allows a screen.

Advantages of 6-0

1.   This system can limit actions between the first and second lines of the attack.
2.   The entire attack happens in front of the defense.

3. The positions and tasks of the defenders are very clear and definite. They vary little during the game.
4. It facilitates the fastbreak because it is often possible to anticipate the actions of the attack.

Disadvantages of 6-0

1. It is difficult to stop shots from far away using this system.
2. It does not work well against teams that move the ball very quickly.
3. When the offense is not very active it is difficult to force a turnover and a low scoring game is likely to result.

These figures will show a few typical tactics for defense 6-0 (See figures 4.23-4.30).

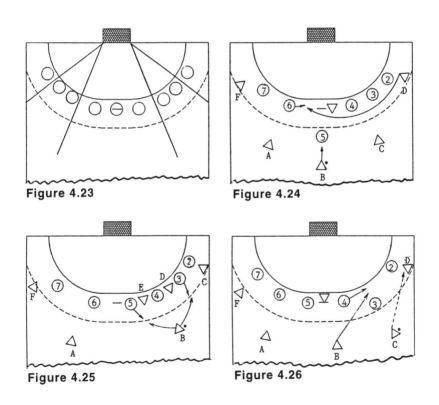

Figure 4.23   Figure 4.24

Figure 4.25   Figure 4.26

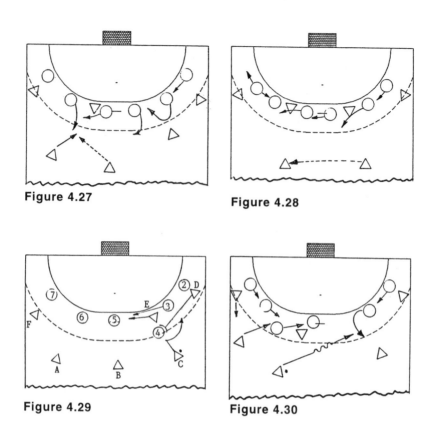

Figure 4.27

Figure 4.28

Figure 4.29

Figure 4.30

GOALKEEPER

The goalkeeper's position is different from all others on the team. The sole function is to block the ball from entering the goal. This position is very strenuous and exhausting. The goalie must be in the ready position with concentration fixed during the entire attack on the goal. During the course of the game, the goalie will have to jump, fall, get up and run in all directions.

Every goalie is unique and should be chosen and developed according to individual characteristics and capabilities. In choosing a goalie, it is important to consider psychological characteristics such as courage and concentration, as well as physical characteristics such as height, length of arms and legs, speed reaction, muscular power, endurance, strength, flexibility and skill. It is especially critical that the goalie not be afraid of contact with the ball or people. Any amount of fear will severely limit the goalie's effectiveness.

There are three fundamentals of goalie play. First, the goalie should position themselves in relationship to the attacker with the ball. Second, the goalie must pay attention and concentrate on the situation, as well as the position of the attacker with the ball. Lastly, the goalie must learn to read the movements of the shooter in order to be able to distinguish which are legitimate shooting movements and which are not.

POSITION

The goalie is constantly aware of the attacker with the ball and positions himself or herself accordingly. With shots from the backcourt or wing shots where the shooter is not jumping into the circle, the goalie should be in the middle of the angle created by a line drawn from the ball to both goal posts. On shots from the 6m line, the goalie should be in the middle of the angle made by drawing a line from the shooting arm of the shooter to the goal posts. At shorter distances, the shooter can greatly vary the shooting angle by changing the position of the ball. Thus, the goalie must choose positioning according to the arm of the attacker, rather than the body in order to decrease the possibility of leaving wide open areas in the goal (See figure 4.31).

Figure 4.31

The goalie's distance from the goal is determined by several factors. First of all, the goalie should choose a distance that feels comfortable. Also, they should vary the distance as much as possible to confuse the shooter, keeping in mind that by moving closer to the shooter the goalie can decrease the effective shooting angle. The normal distance for the goalie to be positioned in front of the goal ranges from 0.5 m (when near the goal post) to 1.5 m (when in the middle of the goal) (See figure 4.32).

Figure 4.32

When the goalie's team is on the attack, they should remain at the 9m line, 2-4 m to the side of the goal. This will enable them to receive passes when necessary to aid the attack and to intercept possible long passes if the other team initiates a fastbreak. In this position, they will still be close enough to the goal to return quickly when necessary.

CONCENTRATION AND ATTENTION

The goalie's job requires an intense amount of energy and concentration. Because of this, the goalie must consciously attempt to conserve energy. They can do this by learning to focus only on the important movements of the attacker with the ball and by learning to relax when the ball is being passed around or when their team is on the attack. The goalie must not direct the defense, but rather concentrate all attention on the ball. Nothing else on the court should be of importance to the goalie.

UNDERSTANDING the SHOOTER

The goalie must learn to study the movement of the shooter to determine where and how to block the shot. One way of doing this is to study the shooter's hand with the ball to determine where the shot will be placed. This method is unreliable since the ball is sometimes behind the shooter prior to the shot and, once the ball is in view, the goalie may not have time to react given the speed of the shot and proximity of the player. The goalie can probably be more effective at blocking shots if they learn to read and analyze the total combination of the shooter's position, gestures and movements prior to the release of the ball. When able to do this, the goalie can learn to anticipate where the shooter is going to throw the ball.

There are several things the goalie can do to improve this ability to anticipate the shooter's actions. First of all, they can study the shooter's habits, including becoming very familiar with the opposing team's statistics prior to the game. Secondly, they must pay attention to the shooter's position in relationship to the goal. For instance, a right-handed shooter on the right side of the goal will often shoot to the right; a left-handed shooter on the left side often shoots to the left. Also, they can study the line of the shoulders to determine the direction of the shot. It is sometimes recommended that the goalie not move until the shooter's hand passes the shoulder line since this is the point at which the shooter becomes committed to the throw and can no longer change the direction of the ball. Lastly, the goalie must consider the height of the ball at the moment of the shot. Statistically, shots made from a low position of the shooter are almost always directed downward.

BASIC POSITION

Ball in the Backcourt: Both feet are on the floor with the weight evenly distributed along the bottom of the feet. The legs are shoulder width apart, no further, as this would be a good target for someone to shoot through. Knees are bent slightly with the head up. The arms are extended out to the sides of the body and slightly bent at the elbow. Hands are facing the court. The goalie may modify this somewhat to achieve the position which is the most comfortable (See figure 4.33).

Ball in the Wing: Both feet are on the floor with the weight evenly distributed. The legs are less bent than above. The leg next to the goalpost is about six inches away to prevent shots from going between the leg and post. The trunk is more upright than mentioned above. The arm nearest the post is in a position with the elbow over

Figure 4.33

the head and the forearm extending over the individual's head with the hand extending out toward the court, taking away the high corner from the shooter. The short corner, or the short part of the angle, is guarded by the goalie's body (figure 4.34). The low corner, or the long angle, is taken away by the goalie's arm and outside leg (see figure 4.35).

Figure 4.34

Figure 4.35

MOVEMENT OF THE GOALIE FOR BLOCKING SHOTS

Goalies should know how to block all types of shots. Following is a description of recommended techniques for blocking specific types of shots. These techniques should be used in conjunction with the goalies natural abilities to achieve the best results. When blocking shots, the goalie should avoid diving for the ball as this takes them out of play when landing on the ground and trying to regain footing. When defending the goal, it can be advantageous for the goalie to vary their technique to keep the shooter from being able to anticipate the goalie's defense. In most situations, the goalie should wait for the shooter to commit himself before moving. This prevents the shooter from being able to change the shot at the last moment and overcome the goalie.

Medium and High Shots: With a shot to the left side of the goal, the weight is on the right leg. The right hand is extended and slightly ahead of the body, attacking the ball. The left hand is extended toward the ball or the high part of the goal to block the shot and the entire body is pushed in the direction of the shot by the opposite leg (See figure 4.36).

Figure 4.36

Low Shots: The weight is on the leg opposite the shot. The leg on the side of the shot is extended as the goalie steps across the goal in the direction of the shot. The hand is over the leg on the side of the shot, slightly bent. The other arm goes over the head in the direction of the shot to help the trunk bend in that direction (See figure 4.37 and 4.38).

Figure 4.37

Figure 4.38

Low Bouncing Shots: The only difference between the movement in this shot and the low shot is that the opposite arm should be extended down between the legs to assist in blocking a ball that may rebound off the leg (See figure 4.39 and 4.40).

Figure 4.39

Figure 4.40

Shots From the Backcourt: The goalie assumes the basic position. As the shot is released, the goalie moves forward diagonally from the goal to attack the ball, using the same technique as outlined above, depending on whether the shot is high, medium, or low.

Shots From the Circle (6m line):

1. The first technique is the same as that outlined above for shots from the backcourt.
2. The second technique consists of a quick step toward the side of the shooter's arm with the closest leg, combined with a sudden lateral movement of the other leg and arm to cover the "long angle". The arm on the side of the shooter's arm goes up from the basic position to cover the short angle.
3. The third technique is the same as for shots from the 7m line.
4. The fourth technique is called the "save going out". For this type of block, the goalie considers the path of the

player in the air and the type of shot that will be attempted. The goalie anticipates where the player will land to shoot. They move there quickly and resumes the basic position with legs together, knees bent slightly and hands ready to attack eminently when the ball is released. As in all shots that are not from the center, the goalie should initiate the outward movement with the foot on the side of the goalpost. This will enable them to better protect the short angle in case of a quick shot while they are initiating the save. This save is different than the others because the goalie begins moving into position for the block prior to determining the trajectory of the ball (See figure 4.41 and 4.42).

Figure 4.41

Figure 4.42

Shots From the Wing, Jumping Into the Goal Area:

1. The first technique involves covering the short angle. The goalie assumes the basic position with their feet near the goal post, covering the short angle. Then waiting for the last movement of the shooter, and moving to block the shot with either the outside arm or leg. The goalie should avoid lifting their foot too soon to prevent the shooter from shooting under the leg (See figure 4.43).

Figure 4.43

2. The second technique involves moving one step laterally to offer the short angle and then moving back to cover that area and stop the shot (See figure 4.44 and 4.45).

3. When the wing has exceptional jumping power enabling them to attain an extreme angle shot, the goalie may use the same techniques for blocking as when someone is shooting from the circle.

Figure 4.44

Figure 4.45

7m Shots: This technique is similar to blocking shots from the center and near the 6m line except that the goalie stands further from the goal to decrease the angle of the shot and increase the possibility of error by the shooter. When offering the shooter the sides of the goal, the goalie should wait until the last moment and surprise the shooter by covering these angles with a sudden jump with both legs and arms open (See figure 4.46).

Figure 4.46

The hand used by the shooter will influence the position of the goalie for blocking this penalty shot attempt. If the shooter is right handed, the goalie will move out from the goal toward the shooter, placing the right shoulder in a direct line with the goal. This allows the left side of the goalie's body to be on the shooter's throwing hand side, offering coverage to that half of the goal. This body positioning by the goalie entices the shooter to use the cross shot to the left-half of the goal to attempt to score. The goalie can cover that shot by quickly moving a few more steps straight forward to cut off the angle of the cross shot to the right side.

TEAM HANDBALL   Skills, Strategies and Training

OFFENSIVE STRATEGIES

INTRODUCTION

This chapter will be devoted to an examination of team handball skills and strategies which contribute to the development of offensive strategy. The fundamentals presented in Chapter Two Basic Playing Skills and Chapter Three Basic Playing Strategies should have provided the foundation necessary to understand and appreciate offensive playing strategy.

SET ATTACK PLAY

The game of team handball parallels the other team sports of soccer and basketball in that the offensive play is organized to create scoring opportunities. The most common method of organizing the offense is with a set attack system. The majority of the actions in attack are in set attack. The old idea of using different phases of attack is now out-dated. Although it may have some usefulness for beginners, it loses its effectiveness for teams involved in high levels of competition.

The objective of set attack is to achieve an optimal shooting position by moving in a strategic manner. It is very important that the attack does not allow the defense to rest. To carry this out effectively, it is necessary to vary the pace of play. When this is done, teams that are poorly prepared will make mistakes that must be capitalized on by the attackers.

All the players must be tactically mature. The overall system of the team must not eliminate the initiative of the players and their individual solutions during the game. The players must be responsible for each action in set attack. Some fundamental rules are set up, but it is up to the players to choose the final solutions. It is the job of the coach to teach them to make the appropriate choices to resolve the different problems that arise during the game. This must be done in practice as well as during competition.

When a team is running a set attack, it is most important that all members contribute to a coordinated attack. When an attacking player draws one defender, they must immediately pass to a teammate who must be prepared to receive the ball. The receiver must be running toward the goal before the passer releases the ball as the receiver will be more dangerous when moving than if stationary. The players must be studying the defensive situation during the entire attack so they will be most effective once they receive the ball. If the defense does not come out, the attacker must attempt to shoot. Each player's action must be subordinate to team play.

NECESSARY ABILITIES

BACK COURT PLAYERS

Back Court players are those offensive players that operate in the area between the goal area line and the free throw line. These players must possess the ability to operate perpendicular to the goal. Because they are constantly on the move, they must be able to fake effectively to both the right and left. These back court players will be taking the majority of the shots. They should master at least two different shots and be proficient passers. They should be able to execute at least three different types of passes to both the center and the second line players. Because they operate in close quarters, first line offensive players must have mastered receiving the ball from every direction and at varying ball speeds. When the front line players possess the skills described above, they will be able to contribute most effectively to the set attack offense.

CIRCLE RUNNERS

Circle runners are those offensive players that primarily operate with their backs to the goal they are attacking. Their role is to continually move from side to side in the area between the goal area line and the free throw line. Their positioning and play must be absolutely subordinate to the needs of team play. The circles' ability to move around and change the pace of the offense are critical in securing a scoring opportunity. This player must be able to use their body to block off defensive players who are trying to disrupt the set pattern attack. The circle is the one offensive player who must communicate to the other teammates regarding screens and picks and other defensive tactics utilized to confuse the offense. Because the circle is one of the first offensive players down the floor, they must be adept in breakaway plays. The player must master shots that can score from one-on-one attempts against the goalkeeper. In some high level offensive systems, teams will use more than one circle runner at the same time. This necessitates a very coordinated effort on the part of the circle runners to keep the offensive pattern operating smoothly.

WINGS

The wings are those offensive players that operate between the goal area line and the free throw line. They are usually positioned out on the sides of the attacking zone. These players stay wide and play deep in the offensive game to help stretch the defense out. This strategy prevents the defense from stacking all the defensive players in the center of the court on the circle runner and center front. In order to be a realistic scoring threat, the wings must constantly move around to draw defensive players with them. This movement, to become a scoring threat, should be so effective that at least two defensive players will have to move to cover the wing.

The wings' ability to receive the ball while constantly moving is a most difficult skill to master. Many hours of practice are necessary to be able to effectively execute at least three kinds of passes, as well as three types of shots. Because the wings take most of their shots from extreme angles to the goal, they must be able to perform simple and double fakes in either direction to get into position to take the shot. Some of their shots require them to dive under the defensive player to get the shot off. This requires a very strong shot to get the ball past the goalie.

OFFENSIVE TACTICAL PROCEDURES

The game of team handball is very similar to basketball in that an organized attack by the offense includes a variety of screens, picks and rolls as well as give and go movements. The ability of all the individual offensive players to carry out their assignments in this type of patterned attack is critical to the overall effectiveness of the total team offense.

SUPPORT POINTS

This is probably the most important procedure of attack in team handball. It consists of consecutive passes and receptions among the attackers, choosing the appropriate paths and the best timing in order to open spots for penetrations or overload situations (more attackers than defenders) anywhere in the offensive zone. What the attackers must try to do is fix defenders, keeping them in places or forcing them to move to the attackers' advantage. They then finish the action of the attack by shooting or passing to the next attacker who will conclude the shot.

CROSSES

This is a tactical procedure where one of the attacking players will invade the position of the other offensive player who crosses out of the area. The perimeter players should try to keep the ball as long as possible before passing to the crossing player. In order to achieve the maximum effect, it is important for the crossing player to isolate their defensive coverage. This will help to create gaps in the total defensive coverage. Because of the close proximity of the crossing players and the other offensive players, it is imperative that passes be short and crisp. After the initial cross, the offensive player whose area has been invaded leaves to fill the attack area of the first player. This crossing effect is intended to confuse the defense and create an open opportunity to score. Offensive players need to be encouraged to make crosses even though they may not receive a pass. The potential to get an open scoring opportunity is why the crossing attack system is so effective (See figure 5.1).

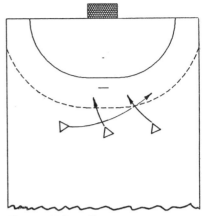

Figure 5.1   Crosses

SCREENS

This procedure consists of standing in front of a defensive player to prevent the player from coming out to defend the shot of an attacking player. Screens are primarily utilized to create shooting opportunities for front line players, although they can be set for any of the other position players as well. In setting screens, two important considerations must be kept in mind. First, the person setting the screen may not use the hands to push against the defender. Secondly, the screener cannot use the arms to hook, hold, or obstruct the defensive player (See figure 5.2).

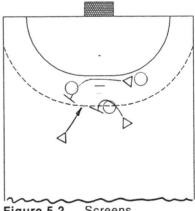

Figure 5.2   Screens

PICKS

This procedure consists of standing on the side of the defensive player to prevent the player from following the offensive player with the ball. This is different from a screen in that the defensive player may be in motion prior to being "picked off" by the attacking player. The player setting the pick can not use the hands or arms against the defender. Timing is very important in setting picks because the attacking players are trying to catch the defensive players by surprise (See figure 5.3).

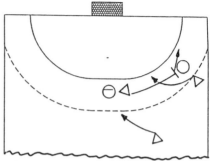

Figure 5.3   Picks

PICK AND ROLL

In this procedure, the offensive player who has set the pick releases after the defensive player has been delayed for a split second in the pursuit of the player with the ball. After releasing the pick, this player rolls back in the direction of the goal to an open area in the defense prepared to receive the quick release pass and shoot. The player with the ball can facilitate the play by faking a shot to the opposite side of the goal before passing to the player who has accomplished the pick and roll. This is intended to draw the goalie out, leaving an open space for the true shot by a teammate (See figure 5.4).

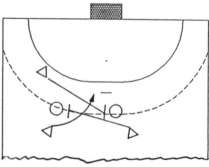

Figure 5.4   Pick and Roll

SWIM MOVE

This offensive tactic starts with the player in possession of the ball positioned about one meter from the defensive player. As soon as the ball is received, the offensive player comes to a jump stop, with the feet approximately shoulder width apart. Holding the ball with both hands, the attacking player strongly fakes first to the non-throwing side, then to the throwing arm side. When the defender reacts to these fakes, the offensive player goes back to the non-throwing side. Before the defender can recover, the offensive player places the non-shooting hand on the defensive player's shoulder to prevent the player from rotating over to stop the attack.

The offensive player, holding the ball in the shooting hand, brings the ball over the head in a swimming stroke motion to get past the defensive player. The placement of the attacker's non-shooting hand on the defender's shoulder and the rotation of the throwing arm into the shooting position occur simultaneously. The right leg of the attacking player steps behind the defensive player, followed by a hop-step to get clear for a shooting opportunity. The action of the arms and legs to get past the defensive player resemble an over hand swimming motion. The key to making this work effectively is for the offensive player to be strong, aggressive and quick to react to actions of the defensive player.

Now that the reader knows the specific functions of the offensive players, we will examine how they will be strategically located on the court to create the variety of offensive systems in team handball.

SPECIFIC OFFENSIVE SYSTEMS

SYSTEM 3-3

This offensive system has three players in the first line (one center, two back court) and three players in the second line (two wings, one circle runner). This system should be used when there are two good shooters who are not creative and need the role of a playmaker to open up the attack. The system 3-3 should also be utilized against an opponent who has a strong defense and well organized fastbreak when passing security is of utmost importance. It facilitates control of all phases of the offense and enables the offense to catch some momentary rest. The 3-3 system is also effective against types of defense systems which leave the center area open, especially the 5+1, 5-1, and the 4-2 (See figure 5.5).

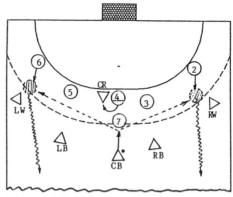

Figure 5.5   System 3-3

This offensive tactic is utilized to encourage errors in the defense play. It is hoped that the crosses, screens and picks will create confusion for the defense and result in open shooting opportunities for the attackers.

In System 3-3, the circle runner should try to operate in the middle of the offense, moving back and forth from the second to the fifth defender. Since the circle runner is one of the first-line players, their major offensive objectives are to penetrate the defense and to be the leader on a fastbreak (See figures 5.6 and 5.7).

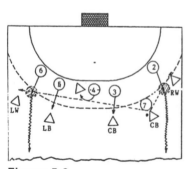

Figure 5.6

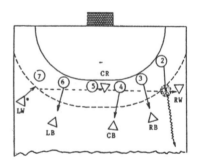

Figure 5.7

When the circle runner moves to the position of being in the middle between the left and right fronts, his or her offensive responsibilities are to make crosses with the other offensive players to create openings in the defense for clear scoring opportunities. The use of the circle runner in opening up offensive options is unlimited. Many teams will utilize two circle runners which allows for many more opportunities to use screens, picks, and pick and rolls to generate scoring opportunities (See figure 5.8).

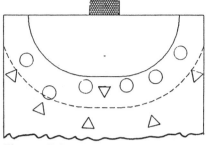

Figure 5.8

The wings' offensive role in the first-line position is to play their specific position deep in the attack zone, to force the defense to cover them. The wings also serve as support points in coordination with the back court. They are able to provide the finishing touches to offensive penetration and getting a shot. The wings' role in the second-line attack position is to assist with the fastbreak, then settle into their regular offensive position. From their regular position the wings can utilize crosses, screens, picks, and pick and rolls to support the offensive attack (See figure 5.9).

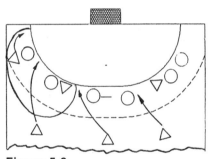

Figure 5.9

When the attacking team switches to a system 3-3 with two circle runners, the second circle runner is one of the wings. This system of attack generates more action and stress on the defense in the center area, but it takes away scoring opportunities from the empty wing area. The use of the double circle runners is very effective against both an open defense and a 5-1 defense (See figure 5.10).

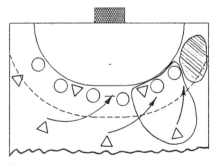

Figure 5.10

Advantages of System 3-3

The advantages of System 3-3 are twofold. First, this system affords much security in movement of the ball. Shorter, direct passes are used primarily, reserving longer passes that could be intercepted for easy breakaways. Secondly, this system creates team cohesion. All six players must work together to create scoring opportunities.

Disadvantages of System 3-3

This system encourages a large number of passes which may result in a slower circulation of the ball with less movement of the defense. Also, problems are created when there are three uncreative shooters on the team. In this case, the offensive players may run the set attack well but are not good at impromptu movements.

SYSTEM 2-4

This system of offense has two players in the first line (two back court) and four players in the second line (two wings, two circles). The main objectives of the system 2-4 are as follows: 1) to break the defense into two blocks; 2) to force the attack into triangles; 3) to help the attackers create a split between the two center defenders; and 4) to encourage a greater interaction with the wings in the total offensive pattern (See figure 5.11).

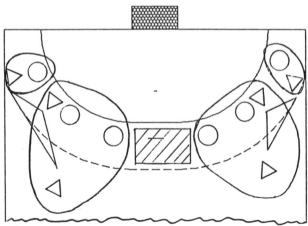

Figure 5.11

The role of the circle runners in this offensive system is to be the primary initiators in the fastbreak attack. They must hustle down the floor to get into a position to be able to start the offensive action. They work together to set screens, picks and pick and rolls to create open scoring opportunities. They also utilize crosses with other second line players to open up lanes for clear shots at the goal. This offensive system should be used when the offensive team has very skilled passers who are also able to successfully utilize fakes in setting up plays. This system of attack can also be used when the attacking team has the ability to shoot well from the outside (See figure 5.12).

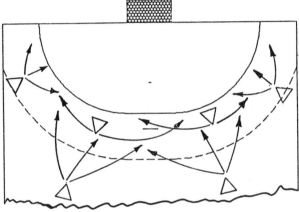

Figure 5.12

Advantages of System 2-4

This system creates an opening in the middle of the defense by cutting the defense into two blocks. The placement of the first and second line players allows for faster movement of the ball from side to side creating open scoring opportunities. This system also generates more overload situations, where the number of attacking players outnumbers the number of defending players. This is most conducive to getting players open for shots.

Disadvantage of System 2-4

The major disadvantage of this attack system is that the attacking players are spread far apart, creating the potential for bad passes and the inability to cover fastbreaks.

SYSTEM 3-3 = 2-4

Now that the strategies of both 3-3 and 2-4 offensive systems is known, it should be noted that during the game, teams normally combine both and switch from one to another. This follows the principle of variation in attack and serves to confuse the defenders.

It is normally the playmaker in the 3-3 system who transforms their position as a first line player into a second-line player (circle runner), momentarily making the defenders change opponents and tasks. After the attack has been completed, he or she returns to position in 3-3 to organize the attack in a different way, perhaps only to return once again to a 2-4 position until an open spot is achieved or an opportunity for scoring becomes available (See figure 5.13).

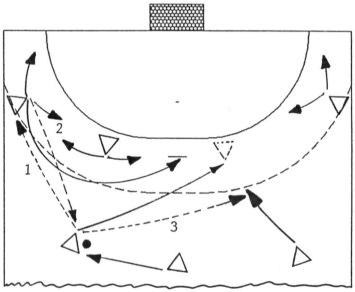

Figure 5.13   System 3-3 = 2-4

This 3-3 = 2-4 can also be attained by transformation of one of the back-courts into a circle runner. This way of playing and switching players from first to second lines can be utilized as a strategy by maintaining the position of the ball and trying the transformation several times. It can also be used as a combination and finalization in a few passes against special situations in defense.

DIFFERENT OFFENSES AGAINST DIFFERENT KINDS OF DEFENSE

In the selection of the offense system to be used against any defense a team must consider several factors before deciding how to attack. It must be aware of the advantages and disadvantages in each offensive and defensive system. The team must study which defensive system they themselves are using. The team must also study the weak points of the system they plan to use. For example, the weak zones, the possible errors that the players may commit, etc. The team must be certain to select an offensive system that takes advantage of its own team's strengths. All offensive players must be able to contribute to the proposed system if it is to be effective in scoring goals.

The coach must present the players with all kinds of problems against different defenses during practise and teach them the different solutions. In the game situation, the coach will be the one to decide the best way to solve the problems in each circumstance.

OFFENSE AGAINST DEFENSE 6-0

The use of either system 3-3 or 2-4 would be effective against the 6-0 defense. There are two general methods that can be used to defeat the 6-0 defense. The first method is to get strong penetration of both wings to serve as support points. As support points, they will cause overloads to create open areas for shots at the goal and effect a quick change in the circulation of the ball to get a player open for a shot. It can be most effective when the wings play deep in the corner and a backcourt player performs a swim move between the wing and #7 or #5 defenders to make a shot or to pass to the wing who will then shoot. (See figure 5.14).

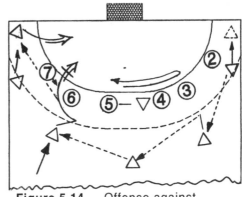

Figure 5.14 Offense against defense 6-0

The second way to beat the 6-0 defense is by having the second line players penetrate the zone. This can be accomplished by either cutting through it or by throwing the ball over the top. In order to cut through the 6-0 defense, the attacking team must make use of effective screens, crosses, picks, and pick and rolls. It must be a total team effort to create the desired effects (See figure 5.15).

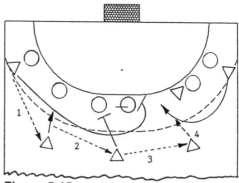

Figure 5.15

OFFENSE AGAINST DEFENSE 5+1

In Defense 5+1, the defense uses one of its better defensive players to put extreme pressure on the ball or on one of the better offensive players. The offense must try to determine quickly if this system is being used by the defense. One method used to determine this is to move a first line player inside as a second line player to see how the defensive team will react. If they follow the player inside they will probably respond with a 6-0 defense. If they do not follow the player to the inside, they will stay 5+1 and go after another one of the strong players (See figure 5.16).

With this specific defense, it is very important for the offense to have a circulation of the wings with the circle

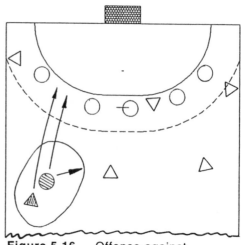

Figure 5.16   Offense against defense 5+1

runners. It is also necessary to coordinate the
crosses between the first-
line players and the circle
runner. This continual
motion creates a pressure
situation for the defense by
forcing them to cover a
designated area, as well as
the switching of players.
This type of moving of-
fense puts a tremendous
amount of pressure on the
defense, hopefully resulting in an open scoring opportunity (See figure 5.17).

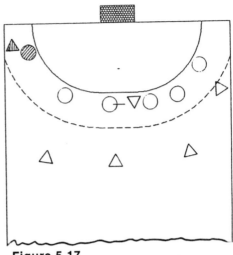

Figure 5.17

FASTBREAK

Much like basketball, team handball situations develop where
there are breakaways resulting with one or more attacking players
against the goal keeper or an offensive number advantage over the
defense. This offensive advantage is usually created by the defense
stealing a pass, blocking a shot, or the offense committing an error in
their attack.

As soon as the shot is made, the direct defender of the shooter
goes into fastbreak. Players on the opposite side do not wait for the
result of the shot. After the stop, the goalie makes a short pass to the
second player and then offers supports outside the circle if necessary.
From there, the rest of the team plays in short passes and triangles
(pass and go), looking for overloads toward the goal. There are also
some areas, after passing midcourt, from which there are no more
passes and the players change pace. They proceed aggressively while
looking for an opportunity to shoot. The situation may be even with
the defenders but the offense has the advantage of the initiative and
the momentum of the run (See figure 5.18).

The main objective of the fastbreak is to create situations of overload. The team must be convinced that situations 2-1 or 3-2 should finish in goals even if the defenders play well. Sometimes the players, coming up against such a situation, lose concentration and make mistakes.

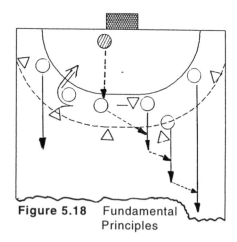

Figure 5.18 Fundamental Principles

FUNDAMENTAL PRINCIPLES

The attacker receiving the ball from the goalkeeper on the initial pass out must not allow the defender to create a foul that results in a free throw. This action will stop any advantage to be gained by the fastbreak. The wings should try to stay wide and maintain depth throughout the break. Attacking players must avoid positioning that places them in a line across the court. This will allow the lone defending player an easier opportunity to guess where the next pass may be made. The breaking players should avoid dribbling the ball unless it is an absolutely secure situation. Generally, passes should be short, accurate set passes rather than slow, inaccurate jump passes. The breaking players should attempt to obtain the perpendicular and central shooting position. In attacking situations where the offense has more players than the defense (2-1, 3-2), they should never execute crosses between themselves because this tends to help the defense cover up easier. The crossing patterns are an excellent tactic to use in even situations (2-2, 3-3) because it forces the defense to cover the crossing players, hoping one will be left uncovered (See figure 5.19).

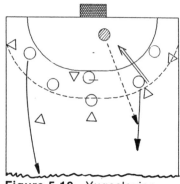

Figure 5.19 Yugoslavian (3-2-1 Defense)

The goalkeeper is a major factor in the fastbreak. They block the shot then must quickly recover the loose ball to make an accurate outlet pass to breaking players. Because of their speed, the wings are usually the first players down court. If the fastbreak does not result in a score, offensive team strategy shifts to the remaining players following the initial break. The trailing players make up the second wave of the attack. These players attempt to attack the defense before they fully recover or organize into some type of patterned defense. When the first and secondary breaks do not result in a goal, then the attacking team assumes their basic positions and initiate a systematic attack (See figure 5.20).

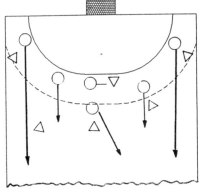

Figure 5.20

TYPES OF FASTBREAKS

Traditional

In this system, the organization for the break is done on the opposite side from where the shot occurred. The wing starts breaking as soon as the shot is taken, not waiting for the results of the shot. The outlet pass from the goalie is critical in getting the fastbreak started. The pass must be strong, accurate, secure, and long enough to hit the streaking wings (See figure 5.21).

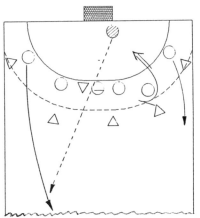

Figure 5.21 Traditional Fastbreak

Czechoslovakian (from 6-0 Defense)

This technique utilizes a predetermined zone to throw the ball into for the fastbreak. That zone could be on the right, center or left side of the court, depending upon where the fastest player is and from which side the attack finished.

For example, the first wave of the break may be initiated by the wing on the opposite side of the shot. Once the break is initiated, the other wing follows quickly down the court. The second wave consists of the players who were located at the six meter line when the shot was taken. The organization of the fastbreak varies with each team according to the skills of the individual players.

Yugoslavian (from 3-2-1 Defense)

This fastbreak is based upon the work of the second defenders and the defender that is out in 9m, trying to stop the shot. They are the first to initiate a fastbreak in case that occurs. The philosophy is that if a defender could not stop the shot and the goalie did, the defender will have to correct that mistake and redeem themselves by scoring on a fastbreak. This fastbreak was invented by Yugoslavia in 1972 because they had the best defenders, and the fastest players in the second position (See figure 5.22).

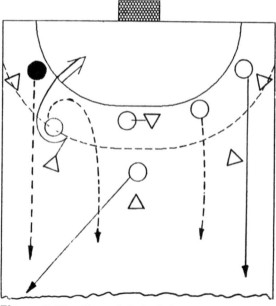

Figure 5.22 From 3-2-1- defense *Note: The solid arrow is the first wave. The dotted arrow is the second wave.*

Polish

The organization and realization of this fastbreak is subordinate to where the shot is coming from. It will start with the second or third player on the opposite side. If the shot comes from the middle, it will start with the second player on either side. The pass from the goalie must be quick and sudden. It must also be short and the player should receive the ball running. After receiving the ball from the goalie, the player should not dribble the ball. Their job is to observe the location of teammates when they are running, and then make a quick, short pass to the player most advantageously located. From here on, players continue with short passes, playing in triangles, looking for overload situations. To finalize the fastbreak, it should be done from the center and normally with a jump shot.

GLOSSARY

A

advantage rule: the referee does not award a free throw or a penalty throw if an interruption of play would be to the disadvantage of the attacking team. The referee will "hold" the whistle, the call being delayed, to determine if play should continue or a free throw or penalty throw should be awarded. This is strictly a judgement call by the referee.

attacking team: the offensive team.

C

center line: the line that divides the court in the center, designate between front court and back court.

charging: the play in which an offensive player runs over a stationary defensive player who has established proper position.

circle: the area contained within the 6 meter line (goal area line) and the goal line. Some-times used to refer to the circle runner on the offensive team.

court players: members of the team actually playing on the court. All players except the goalkeeper. There are usually 6 court players.

D

diving shot: a means of trying to score a goal by launching the entire body into the air toward the goal in an attempt to gain more distance. The ball must be released before the body touches the ground inside the goal area line.

dual refereeing system: the use of two referees in a game. The usual positions are for one to be at the center and the other to be down on the goal line.

F

first line: the offensive players that play the back-court.

free throw: the method of putting the ball back into play after a minor foul, violation, or an infraction of the rules.

free throw line: the broken line drawn parallel to the goal area line at an extra distance of 3 meters, the 9m line. This line is used for taking free throws for minor fouls that occur between the 6m and the 9m lines. The ball is put into play from the 9m line directly opposite from the foul or violation.

G

goal: a goal refers to the unit of scoring as well as the area/ structure the ball must pass into in order to score. A goal is scored when the ball has passed wholly over the goal line between the up-rights and underneath the crossbar of the goal.

goal area: the area of the playing court inside and including the goal area line (6 meter line). This area is restricted to the goalkeeper.

goal area line: the line which is drawn in the shape of a **D** at a distance of 6 meters in front of an on either side of the goal. It is also referred to as the 6 meter line.

goal keeper: the player who is allowed to play freely inside the goal area with the specific responsibility of defending the goal.

goal line: the line that extends the width of the court at each end of the court. The line is 5 cm (2 in) wide except in front of the goal, where the line is 8 cm (4 in) wide.

goal throw: a method of restarting play after the ball has been deflected by the goalkeeper or thrown by the attacking team over the goal line without going into the goal. Only the goalkeeper may put the ball into play by throwing the ball from the goal area out into the playing area. In some areas this is also referred to as a throw-out.

J

jump shot: a shot at the goal taken when the attacking player is in the air above the defending players or jumping from outside the 6 meter line to get as close to the goal as possible before releasing the ball.

M

marking: this is a tactic used by a player to prevent the opposing player from breaking through the defense or making a shot. The defense may legally use their body to obstruct a player with or without the ball. Also referred to as "checking".

P

penalty line: a line one meter in length parallel to the goal line and 7 meters away from the goal.

penalty throw: a shot awarded to an offensive player when any offensive player is prevented from making a clear goal-scoring chance by a major foul. The player attempting the penalty throw is required to make a direct shot to score a goal from the penalty line.

playing court: the area within the lines marking the perimeter of the player area.

R

referees throw: the court referee shall throw the ball vertically up in the air to restart the game after an interruption of play caused by players of both teams committing simultaneous infractions of the rules or if the game has been interrupted, for some reason, without any infractions of the rules being committed. This is similar to a jump ball in basketball.

S

second line: the offensive players that play along the circle, which usually includes the wings and the circle runners.

seven meter line: also known as the penalty line.

substitution: the changing of one player for another while the game is in progress.

substitution area: the designated area 4.5 meters on either side of the center line where substitutes are required to enter and leave the playing court.

suspension: a period of time in which a player is ordered, by the referee, temporarily out of the game. This is for a period of 2 minutes:

T

throw in: the method of putting the ball back into play after it has crossed one of the side lines. The throw is taken by a player of the team which did not cause the ball to go out. The player making the throw must have one foot in constant contact with the side line while the throw is being made. They may throw the ball into the playing area in any manner.

throw off: the method of putting the ball into play at the start of the game and after a goal is scored. The throw is made from the center of the court.

throw out: the same as a Goal Throw.

REFERENCES

1985 Edition. *International Handball Federation Rules of the Game*

Cavanaugh, Michael D. *IHF Coaching Symposium.*

Cavanaugh, Michael D. *Team Handball in Physical Education for High School Students.*

Dewight, Maryphyl and Kate McRae. *This is Team Handball.*

Garcia Cuesta, Javier. *Handball Tactics.*

Grage, Werner. *Super-Handball-Training.* 1990.

Singer, Erwin. *Hallen Handball.* Stuttgart, 1983.

RULES
INTERNATIONAL HANDBALL
FEDERATION (IHF)

Rule 1   The Playing Area

1:1   The full sized court (figure 1.1, page 5) is a rectangle of 40 m
         length and 20 m width. The length has the side lines, the width
         goal lines (outer plus inner goal lines). It consists of a playing
         area divided into two halves by a center line parallel to the goal
         lines, and two goal areas.

         The conditions of the playing area dimensions and the surface must
         not be altered in any way such that one team gains an advantage.

1:2   The Goal (figure 1.2, page 6).

         Each goal must be placed centrally on its respective outer goal
         line. Each goal is two meters high and three meters wide (inner
         measures).

         The goal posts must be firmly attached to the ground and joined
         by a horizontal crossbar. The back edge of the goal-posts shall
         be in line with the outer edge of the goal line. The goal-posts and
         crossbar must be 8 cm x 8 cm cross section and must be of the
         same material (e.g. wood, light metal, or synthetic material). They
         must be painted on all sides in contrasting bands of two colors
         which contrast effectively with the background.

         Where the goal posts and crossbar join, they shall be painted in
         the same color from each end 28 cm long. All other rectangles
         of color shall be 20 cm long (figure 1.2, page 6). The goal shall
         have a net attached to it in such a way that a ball thrown into
         it cannot rebound immediately.

1:3   The goal area is marked with a line 3 meters long parallel to and
         6 meters from the goal line, equidistant from the side lines. (Mea-
         surements include the thickness of all lines). The ends of this line
         are joined to the goal line by means of two quarter circles each
         having a radius of 6 meters measured from the near inner corner
         of the goal-posts (figure 1.2 page 6). This complete line is known
         as the goal area line and its outer edge defines the goal area (figure
         1.1, page 5).

1:4   The free-throw (9 meter) line is a broken line, where both the solid
         lines and spaces between them, measure 15 cm, drawn 3 meters
         beyond and parallel to the goal line (figure 1.1, page 5).

1:5	The 7-m-line is 1 m long, and is parallel to and 7 m from the rear end of the goal line, centrally placed between the side lines.
1:6	The goalkeeper's border line is 15 cm long, and is parallel to and 4 m from the rear end of the goal line, centrally placed between the side lines.
1:7	The center line connects the center points of the two side lines (figure 1.1, page 5).
1:8	The substitution lines shall be defined by a line 15 cm long line either side of the center line, each line to be constructed on the course at right angles to the side line and 4.50 meters away from the center line (figure 1.1, page 5).
1:9	All lines form part of the area which they enclose. They shall be 5 cm wide (except 1:10) and clearly visible.
1:10	The inner goal-lines shall be 8 cm wide to coincide with the goal-post (figure 1.4, page 11).

Rule 2   Playing Time

2:1	The playing time shall be two 30 minute periods with an interval of 10 minutes between for all male and female teams whose players are 18 years or older.
2:2	The playing time begins with the court referee's whistle for the throw-off, and ends with the timekeeper's final signal.
	Infringements and acts of unsporting conduct committed before a timekeeper's signal must still be punished by the referees even after this signal is given. The court referee only ends the period of play after the necessary free-throw or penalty has taken place and its result ascertained.
2:3	The teams change ends for the second period of play.
2:4	The referees decide if and when the playing time is to be interrupted and when it is to be restarted.
	They will signal to the time-keeper when the timing clock must be stopped (time-out) and restarted.
	Interruption of playing time - time-out - is to be indicated to the time-keeper by three short blasts on the whistle and the "T" sign.
	The whistle must always be blown to indicate resumption of the game after time out (16:3a)

2:5   If just before the end of a period of play a free-throw or a penalty is awarded, the time-keeper must wait for the immediate result of this throw before blowing the final signal, even if the playing time has already run out (19:5).

2:6   If the referees decide that the time-keeper has ended playing too early, they must keep the players on the court and play the rest of the time.

The team which was put at a disadvantage through the incorrect blowing of the final whistle shall remain in possession of the ball.

If the first half has been terminated too late, the second half must be shortened accordingly.

2:7   If a game is tied at the end of normal time, where the rules of the competition demand a winner to be determined, a toss of a coin after a five minute interval determines which side has the throw off or choice of ends.

The period of extra time will be 2 x 5 minutes (change ends at half time with no interval) for all teams.

If the game is still tied following the extra time, a second period of extra time shall be played after a five minute interval and a new coin shall be tossed. The second extra time consists of two five minute periods of play with no half time interval.

If the game is still tied after the second extra time, the rules of the competition will be applied to decide the winner.

Rule 3 The Ball

3:1   The ball must be produced by leather or a synthetic material. It must be spherical. The surface must not be shiny or slippery (18:3).

3:2   The ball measured at the start of play must have a circumference of 58-60 cm and a weight of 425-475 g for men.

For ladies the ball must have a circumference of 54-56 cm and weight 325-400 g.

3:3   There must be two balls conforming to the rules available for every game.

3:4   Once the game has started, the selected ball shall be changed only for reasons of absolute necessity.

3:5   Only balls marked with the official I.H.F. logo shall be used for international events and international games (section IX of the I.H.F. statutes).

Rule 4 The Players

4:1   A team consists of 12 players (10 court players and 2 goal-keepers), who must be listed on the score sheet.

The team must use a goal-keeper at all times.

No more than 7 players (6 court players and 1 goal-keeper) may be present on the court at any time. The remaining players are substitutes.

Only the substitutes and any suspended players, plus 4 officials, are allowed in the substitution area (figure 1.1 page 5).

The officials must be listed on the scoring sheet, and one of them appointed as responsible for his team. Only this official has the right to address himself to the score-taker/time-keeper and, if necessary, the referees.

4:2   Both teams must have at least 5 players on court at the start of the game, one of whom must be listed on the score sheet as a goal-keeper.

At any time during the game, including extra-time, the number of players in the team can be increased up to a maximum of 12.

The game may continue even if a team is reduced to less than 5 players.

4:3   A players is eligible to play if he is included on the score sheet and present at the start of the game.

A player who is entitled to play may enter the court at any time over this team's substitution line.

Players who arrive after the game has started must receive permission to play from the score-taker/time-keeper.

If a player who is not eligible to play enters the court, the opposing team shall be awarded a free-throw, and the player shall be disqualified (17:5 a).

4:4   Substitutes may enter the game at any time without notifying the score-taker/time-keeper, as long as the players they are replacing have already left the court (4:5).

This also applies to the substitution of goal-keepers.

All players shall leave or enter the court only over their own team's substitution line (4:5, 13:1a).

During time out the court may only be entered additionally from the substitution area with the permission of a referee (signals 18 and 19).

4:5   A foul substitution shall be penalized by a free-throw (13:1a) to be taken from the place where the substitute entered the court. In addition the entering player shall be suspended for 2 minutes (17:3a). If the foul substitu-tion takes place during a stoppage of the game, the player shall also be suspended for 2 minutes, and the game restarted by the throw appropriate to the original stoppage.

If there is any pronounced unsporting conduct or assault, either in connection with or following the foul substitution, the guilty player shall be disqualified or excluded respectively (17:5d, 17:7).

4:6   If an extra player enters the court against the rules, he shall be suspended for 2 minutes and another player must leave the court for him for 2 minutes.

If a suspended player enters the court during his period of suspension, he shall be suspended for an additional period of 2 minutes and another player must leave the court for the rest of his suspension time.

The team official must decide which other player is to leave the court. In case of his refusal to decide, the referees shall decide who is to leave the court.

4:7   All the court players in a team shall wear identical uniforms, but contrasting to the uniforms of both teams' goal-keepers (18:3).

The players shall be numbered from 1 to 20, numbers 1, 12 and 16 being reserved for goal-keepers. The players shall have numbers on the back of their shirts, at least 20 cm high, and on the front, at least 10 cm high.

The color of the numbers must contrast with the color of the uniforms.

The players shall wear sports shoes.

Bracelets, watches, rings, necklaces/chains, earrings, glasses without rims or fastenings, and any other items which could be dangerous to the players are prohibited (18:3). Players who do not meet these requirements will not be allowed to take part until the offending articles have been removed.

The captain of each team must wear an armlet on an upper arm, which should be approximately 4 cm wide, and must contrast with the color of the shirt.

Rule 5   The Goal-Keeper

5:1   A goal-keeper must never replace a court player. A court player, however, may replace a goal-keeper.

The score-taker/time-keeper must be informed if a goal-keeper is to be replaced by a court player (17:3a).

The court player must change uniform before he replaces the goal-keeper via the substitution area (4:7).

The goal-keeper is **permitted** to:

5:2   touch the ball with any part of his body when in the act of defense inside the goal area.

5:3   move around with the ball inside the goal area without any restriction, (see, however, 16:3b).

5:4   leave the goal area without being in possession of the ball and participate in the game in the playing area. In the playing area the goalkeeper is subject to the rules applying to the court players (see, however, 5:12).

The goal-keeper is considered to have left the goal area as soon as any part of his body touches the ground outside the goal area line.

5:5   leave the goal area with the ball and play it again in the playing area, if in the act of defending he has not managed to get the ball completely under control.

The goal-keeper is **not permitted** to:

5:6   endanger an opponent whilst in the act of defense (8:12).

5:7   intentionally play the ball over his own outer goal line once he has got the ball under control (13:1b).

5:8   leave the goal area with the ball under his control (13:1b).

5:9   touch the ball outside the goal area after a goal throw unless it has touched another player in between (13:1b).

5:10   touch the ball while it is stationary or rolling on the ground outside the goal area line while he is inside the goal area (13:1b).

5:11   take the ball into the goal area when it is stationary or rolling on the ground outside the goal area line (14:1b).

5:12   re-enter the goal area from the playing area whilst in possession of the ball, (14:1b).

5:13   touch the ball with his feet or legs below the knees while it is moving towards the playing area, or when it is stationary in the goal area (13:1b).

5:14   touch or cross the goal-keeper's border line (4 meter line), or its projection to either side, before the ball has left the thrower's hand when a penalty throw is being taken (14:8).

Rule 6   The Goal Area

6:1   Only the goal-keeper is allowed to enter the goal area (see, however, 6:3). The goal area, which includes the goal area line, is regarded as entered when a court player touches it with any part of his body.

6:2   When a court player enters the goal area the following decisions shall be taken:

    a) free-throw, if the court player enters the goal area while in possession of the ball (13:1c);

    b) free-throw, if a court player enters the goal area while not in possession of the ball and thereby gains an advantage (13:0c, see, however, 6:2c);

    c) penalty-throw, if by entering the goal area a defending player gains an advantage over an attacking opponent who is in possession of the ball (14:1c).

6:3   A court player who enters the goal area shall not be penalized:

    a) if he enters the goal area after playing the ball, as long as this causes no disadvantage to the opponent;

    b) if he enters the goal area without the ball and thereby gains no advantage;

    c) if he is in defense and enters the goal area during or after an attempt to defend without causing a disadvantage for the opponent.

6:4   When the ball is inside the goal area it belongs to the goal-keeper.

    No court player shall be allowed to touch the ball when it is stationary or rolling on the goal area's ground or when it is in the goal-keeper's possession (13:1c). It is permitted to play the ball when it is in the air above the goal area.

6:5   When the ball ends up in the goal area, the goal-keeper shall put it back into play.

6:6   Play shall continue if in the act of defense a player of the defending team touches the ball, which thereafter is taken by the goal-keeper, or comes to rest in the goal area.

6:7   If a player intentionally plays the ball into his own goal area the referee shall decide as follows:

    a) Goal, if the ball goes entirely into the goal;

    b) Penalty-throw, if the goal-keeper touches the ball and it does not go into the goal (14:1d);

    c) Free-throw, if the ball comes to rest inside the goal area or goes over the outer goal line (13:1e);

    d) Play continues, if the ball traverses the goal area without having been touched by the goal-keeper.

6:8   A ball which returns from the goal area out into the playing area remains in play.

Rule 7 Playing the Ball

A player is **permitted:**

7:1   to throw, catch, stop, push, hit or throw the ball with his hands (open or closed), by using hands, arms, head, torso, thighs and knees;

7:2   to hold the ball for a maximum of 3 seconds, even when it is lying on the ground;

7:3   to take a maximum of three steps with the ball. One step is considered taken when:

    a) a player who is standing with both feet on the ground lifts one foot and puts it down again, or moves one foot from one place to another;

    b) if a player who touches the ground with one foot only, catches the ball and then touches the ground with the other foot;

    c) if a player, after a jump, touches the ground with one foot only and then hops on the same foot or touches the ground with the other foot;

    d) if a player, after a jump, touches the ground with both feet simultaneously and then lifts one foot and puts it down again, or moves one foot from one place to another.

7:4   While standing or running:

    a) to bounce the ball once and catch it again with one or both hands;

    b) to bounce the ball repeatedly with one hand (i.e. dribble the ball), or to roll the ball on the ground repeatedly with one hand, and thereafter catch it or pick it up again with one or both hands.

As soon as the ball is held in one or both hands, it must be played within 3 seconds or after no more than 3 steps.

The bouncing or dribbling the ball only starts when the player touches the ball with any part of his body and then directs it towards the ground.

When the ball has touched another player or the goal, the player is allowed to tap, bounce and catch it again.

7:5   to move the ball from one hand into the other one;

7:6   to play the ball while kneeling, sitting or laying on the ground.

A player is **not permitted:**

7:7   to touch the ball more than once, unless it has touched the ground, another player, or the goal (13:1d)

Fumbling shall not be penalized.

7:8   to touch the ball with his feet or legs below the knees (13:1d), except when the ball has been thrown at the player by an opponent.

This infringement shall, however, not be penalized if it does not lead to an advantage for the player or his team;

7:9   to dive for the ball when it is stationary or rolling on the ground (13:1d).

This rule does not apply to the goal-keeper when he is in his own goal area;

7:10   to play the ball intentionally over the side lines or the outer goal line (13:1e).

This rule does not apply to the goal- keeper in the goal area when he fails to get the ball under control and directs it over his own outer goal line (goal-throw);

7:11   to keep the ball in the team's possession without making any recognizable attempt to attack or to try to score a goal. This is passive play and is to be penalized by a free-throw from the spot where the ball was when play was interrupted (13:1f).

7:12   Play continues if the ball touches a referee on the playing court.

Rule 8   The Approach to the Opponent

A player is **permitted:**

8:1   to use his hands and arms to gain possession of the ball;

8:2   to use an open hand to play the ball from an opponent in any direction.

8:3   to obstruct an opponent with the torso even if the opponent is not in possession of the ball.

A player is **not permitted:**

8:4   to obstruct an opponent with arms, hands or legs;

8:5   to push an opponent into the goal area;

8:6   to pull or hit the ball with one or both hands out of the opponent's hand(s);

8:7   to use the fist to play the ball from an opponent;

8:8   to endanger an opponent with the ball, or to move the ball towards the opponent in a dangerous feint;

8:9   to endanger the goal-keeper;

8:10   to hold an opponent with one or both arms, or to push him;

8:11   to run into, to jump into, to trip up, to hit or to threaten an opponent in any other way.

8:12   Fouls regarding the approach to the opponent (5:6, 8:4-11) shall be penalized by a free-throw (13:1g) or a penalty throw (14:1a, 17:1a).

8:13   Fouls regarding the approach to the opponent (8:4-11) where the action is mainly or exclusively directed at the opponent and not at the ball are to be penalized progressively (17:1b, 17:3b). Progressive penalization also applies to unsporting conduct (17:1d, 17:3c).

8:14   Serious fouls regarding the approach to the opponent or pronounced unsporting conduct shall be penalized by disqualification of the guilty player (17:5b, 17:5d).

8:15   A player guilty of assault on the court shall be excluded (17:7).

Rule 9 Scoring

9:1   A goal is scored when the whole of the ball has crossed the inner goal line (Figure 1.4, page 11), provided that no in-fringement of the rules has been committed by the scoring player or any player of his team prior to, or after his throw.

        when a defending player commits an infringement of the rules in an attempt to prevent the scoring, but the ball still goes into the goal, the goal shall be awarded.

        If a referee or the time-keeper has blown his whistle before the whole of the ball has crossed the inner goal line, the goal cannot be counted.

        An own goal, whereby a defender puts the ball into his own goal, shall count as a goal for the opponents, unless the ball has previously crossed the outer goal line.

9:2   If the referees have allowed a goal and have blown the whistle for the subsequent throw-off, the goal cannot be disallowed any longer.

9:3   The team which has scored more goals than the other is the winner.

9:4   The game shall be declared a draw if both teams have scored the same number of goals or no goals at all.

Rule 10 Throw-Off

10:1   The throw-off at the start of the game shall be taken by the team which wins the coin toss and chooses to start in possession of the ball, or the team whose opponents win the coin toss and opt to choose ends.

The throw-off at the start of the second half shall be taken by the other team.

A new coin toss is made before any extra time.

10:2   After a goal has been scored, play is resumed by a throw-off taken by the team which conceded the goal.

10:3   The throw-off shall be taken from the center of the court in any direction. After the referee has blown his whistle the throw-off must be taken within three seconds (13:1h).

10:4   All players shall be in their own half of the court when the throw-off is taken, and the opponents shall be at least 3 meters away from the player taking the throw-off (13:1h).

Rule 11 Throw-In

11:1   A throw-in is awarded if the whole of the ball crosses the side line, or if a court player of the defending team last touched the ball before it crossed the outer goal line (see, however, 7:10).

11:2   The throw-in is taken without any whistle signal from the referee, (see, however, 16:3b) by a player from that team whose players did not touch the ball last before it crossed the side line or outer goal line.

11:3   The throw-in is to be taken from the place where the ball crossed the side line or from the end of the side line on that side of the goal where the ball crossed the outer goal line.

11:4   The player taking the throw-in must have one foot on the side line until the ball has left his hand.

The same player is not allowed to put the ball on the ground and then to pick it up again or to dribble it and catch it again (13:1i).

11:5   Whilst the throw-in is being taken, the opponents must stay at least 3 meters from the thrower.

However, they are, in any situation, allowed to stand immediately outside their goal area line, even if the distance from them to the thrower is less than 3 meters.

Rule 12 Goal-Throw

12:1   A goal-throw shall be awarded when the ball crosses the outer goal line (see, however, 5:7, 7:10).

12:2   A goal-throw is to be taken from the goal area over the goal area line without any whistle signal from the referee (see, however, 16:3b).

The goal-throw is considered taken when the ball thrown by the goal-keeper has crossed the goal area line.

12:3   If the ball comes to rest in the goal area, the goal-keeper shall bring the ball back into play (see, however, 6:7c).

12:4   The goal-keeper must not touch the ball again after his goal-throw until it has touched another player, (5:9, 13:1k).

Rule 13 Free-Throw

13:1   A free-throw is awarded in the case of:
  a) incorrect substitution or entering the court against the rules (4:4-6);
  b) infringements by the goal-keeper (5:7-10, 5:13);
  c) infringements by court players in the goal area (6:2 a-b, 6:4);
  d) playing the ball incorrectly (7:2-4, 7-9);
  e) deliberately playing the ball across the outer goal line or side line (6:7s, 7:10;
  f) passive play (7:11);
  g) fouls concerning the approach to opponents (8:12);
  h) infringement in connection with a throw-off (10:3-4);
  i) infringement in connection with a throw-in (11:4);
  k   infringement in connection with a goal-throw (12:4);
  l) infringement in connection with a free-throw (13:3);
  m) interruption of play without infringement of the rules (13:7);
  n) infringement in connection with penalty throw (14:2-4, 6);
  o) infringement in connection with a referee's throw (15:3);
  p) incorrect taking of throws (16:2-5);
  q) unsporting conduct (8:13-14);
  r) assault (8:15).

13:2   The free-throw is principally taken without any whistle signal from the referee (see, however, 16:3 a-h) generally from the place where the infringement occurred.

If a free-throw is awarded to the attacking team and the infringement occurred between the goal area line and the free-throw line of the defending team, the free-throw shall be taken from the nearest point outside the free-throw line.

13:3   Once an attacking player is with the ball in the correct position, he may not dribble the ball, or put it down and pick it up again (13:1l).

13:4   Players of the attacking team must not touch or cross their opponent's free-throw line while a free-throw is taken (16:3c).

The referees must correct the positions of players of the attacking team who are inside the free-throw line when a free-throw is being taken if the incorrect positions might interfere with the game.

The free-throw shall then be taken following the whistle signal.

13:5   When a free-throw is taken, the opponents must remain at a distance of at least 3 meters. However, they may stand immediately outside their goal area line, if the free-throw is being taken on their free-throw line.

13:6   The referee must not award a free-throw in the event of an infringment by a defending team where this would lead to a disadvantage for the attacking team.

Where an infringement causes the attacking team to loose possession of the ball, a free-throw must be awarded at least.

If, in spite of the infringement, the attacking player retains full control of both ball and body, a free-throw should not be awarded.

13:7   In the event of the game being interrupted without any infringement of the rules and one team being in possession of the ball, the game shall be restarted by that team from the place where the ball was at the interruption with a free-throw or the required throw at a whistle signal from the referee (13:1m, 16:3a).

13:8   The ball must be put down immediately by the player who is in possession of the ball if a decision is called against his team (17:3d).

Rule 14 Penalty-Throw

14:1   A penalty-throw shall be awarded:

   a)   When a clear chance of scoring is spoilt by an infringement in any part of the court, even when committed by an official;
   b)   When a goal-keeper enters his goal area with the ball, or takes it into the goal area (5:11-12);
   c)   When a court player enters his own goal area to gain an advantage over an attacking opponent who is in possession of the ball (6:2c).
   d)   When a court player intentionally plays the ball to his own goal-keeper in the goal area (6:7b);

14:2   The penalty-throw is to be taken as a shot towards the goal within 3 seconds after the whistle signal from the court referee (13:1n).

14:3   The player taking the penalty-throw must not touch or cross the penalty-throw line before the ball has left his hand (13:1n).

14:4   Once the penalty throw has been taken the ball may not be played until it has touched the goal-keeper or the goal (13:1n).

14:5   Whilst the penalty-throw is being taken, players, with the exception of the player taking the throw, are not allowed to stand between the goal-area line and the free-throw line.

14:6   If a player of the attacking team touches or crosses the free-throw line before the ball has left the thrower's hand, a free-throw shall be awarded to the defending team (13:1n).

14:7   Whilst the penalty throw is being taken, all players of the defending team must stand at least 3 meters from the thrower. If a player of the defending team touches or crosses the free-throw line or steps nearer than 3 meters to the thrower before the ball has left the thrower's hand, the referees shall decide as follows:

        a)   Goal, if the ball goes into the goal.

        b)   Repetition of the penalty throw in all other cases.

14:8   If while a penalty throw is being taken, the goal-keeper touches or crosses the goal-keeper's border line - 4 meter line - (1:6, 5:14) before the ball has left the thrower's hand, the penalty-throw shall be retaken, if no goal has been scored.

14:9   The referees must not award a penalty-throw for an infringement by the defending team if this would be disadvantageous to the attacking team.

        When a clear chance of scoring is denied to the extent that no goal is scored, at least a penalty-throw must be awarded.

        If, in spite of the infringement, the attacking player retains full control of both ball and body, a penalty-throw should not be awarded.

Rule 15 Referee's Throw

15:1   The game shall be re-started by a referee's throw if:

        a)   Players of both teams infringed the rules simultaneously;
        b)   The ball touches the ceiling or any fixed equipment attached above the playing court;
        c)   The game was interrupted, without any infringement of the rules committed, and no team being in possession of the ball.

15:2 The court referee shall throw the ball vertically up in the air, without a whistle signal, at the place where the ball was when play was interrupted.

If this play is between the goal area line and the free-throw line or above the goal area, the referee's throw shall be taken from the nearest spot directly outside the free-throw line.

The referee's throw is taken after a whistle signal if there has been time out (16:3a).

15:3 While the referee's throw is being taken, all players with the exception of one from each time, must remain at a distance of at least 3 meters from the referee who is taking the throw, (13:1o).

Both the players who are jumping for the ball shall stand next to the referee, each on the side nearest to his own goal.

The ball may only be played when it has passed its highest point (13:1o).

Rule 16 Taking the Throws

16:1 Before a throw is taken, the ball must be held in the thrower's hand. All players must taken a position on the court in accordance with the rules on the throw in question, (see, however, 16:7).

16:2 When taking a throw-off, throw-in, free-throw or penalty-throw, the thrower must keep one part of a foot in constant contact with the ground (13:1p). The player may, however, lift and put down the other foot repeatedly.

16:3 The referee must whistle:

a) When the game is re-started (2:4, 10:3, 13:7, 14:2, 15:2);
b) When taking of a throw-in, a goal-throw or free-throw is delayed, (11:2, 12:2, 13:2);
c) after a correction or a caution (13:4, 16:7);
d) after a warning (17:1);
e) after a suspension (17:3);
f) after a disqualification (17:5);
g) after an exclusion (17:7);
h) when the referees disagree as to which team shall be penalized (18:9).

The thrower must play the ball within 3 seconds after the whistle being blown (13:1p).

16:4 A throw is considered taken when the ball has left the hand of the thrower (see, however, 12:2, 15:3).

When taking the throw, the player must actually throw the ball. It cannot be handed to nor touched by a teammate (13:1p).

16:5   The player taking the throw must not touch the ball again until it has touched another player or the goal (13:1P).

16:6   A goal may be scored directly from any throw (see, however, 9:1).

16:7   When a throw-in or a free-throw is to be taken, the referees must not correct incorrect positions of the defending team when the attacking team suffers no disadvantage by throwing immediately. If it is at a disadvantage, the incorrect position must be corrected (16:3).

If the referee blows his whistle for a throw to be taken despite of incorrect positions on the part of the defenders, those defenders are fully entitled to interfere and must not be penalized.

If the opponent delay or interfere with the taking of a throw by standing too close or infringing the rules in some other way, he shall be warned, and if he repeats the offense he shall be suspended (17:1c, 17:3c, see, however, 12:2).

Rule 17 The Punishments

17:1   A warning can be given for:

a) fouls concerning the approach to an opponent (5:6, 8:4-11);

A warning shall be given for:

b) fouls concerning the approach to an opponent to be punished progressively (8:13);
c) fouls when the opponent is taking a throw (16:7);
d) unsporting conduct by a player or official (17:11, 17:12 a and c).

17:2   When a warning is given, the referee shall indicate this to the guilty player or official and to the scoretaker/time-keeper by holding up the yellow card.

17:3   A suspension shall be given:

a) for incorrect substitution or entering the court against the rules (4:4-6);
b) for repeated foul concerning the approach to the opponent to be punished progressively (8:13);
c) for repeated unsporting conduct by a player on the court (8:13, 17:11);
d) if the ball is not put down immediately by the player in possession of it when the decision goes against his team (13:8);
e) for repeated infringements of the rules when the opponent is taking throws (16:7).

In exceptional cases a suspension can be given without any previous warning.

17:4   A suspension shall be clearly indicated to the player concerned and to the score-taker/time-keeper by the official hand-signal (one arm raised in the air with two fingers extended).

Suspension is always imposed for a playing time of 2 minutes; if the same player is suspended a third time, he will be disqualified (17:5 e).

During the time of suspension, the suspended player is not allowed to participate and his team is not allowed to be completed.

The period of suspension begins when play is restarted by the whistle.

If a player's suspension time has not expired by the end of the first half, it is carried over to the second half. The same applies to extra time.

17:5   A disqualification shall be given:

a)   if a player who is not entitled to take part enters the court (4:3);
b)   for serious fouls regarding the approach to an opponent (8:14);
c)   repeated unsporting conduct by an official or a player outside the court (17:11, 17:12d);
d)   pronounced unsporting conduct (8:14), also by an official (17:11, 17:12b and c);
e)   for a third suspension (17:4);
f)   for assaults by an official or a player outside the court.

Disqualification of a player on the court is always accompanied by a period of suspension.

17:6   A disqualification is after a time-out to be indicated to the guilty player and to the score-taker/time-keeper by the holding up of a red card.

A disqualification of a player or an official always applies to the remaining playing time. The player or the official must leave the court as well as the substitution area immediately.

When a player is disqualified, the number of players available to a team is reduced by one (except 17:12b). A team, however, may continue to play at full strength on the court after the expiry of the suspension time.

17:7   An exclusion shall be given:

In the event of an assault on the court (8:15, 17:9).

17:8 The exclusion is, after a time out, to be indicated directly to the guilty player, his responsible team official and to the score-taker/time-keeper.

The referee signals the exclusion of a player by crossing his arms at head-height.

An exclusion always applies to the remaining playing time.

The excluded player may not be replaced and must leave the court as well as the substitution area immediately.

17:9 If a player who has been suspended commits an assault on the court, he shall be excluded. If he shows pronounced unsporting conduct or is guilty of an assault in the substitution area, he shall be disqualified.

17:10 If a goal-keeper is suspended, disqualified or excluded, he may be replaced by the substitute goal-keeper. In this case a court player must leave the court in his place.

17:11 A player who is guilty of unsporting conduct shall be warned by the referees (17:1d), whether he is on or off the court.

If the offense is repeated, the player shall be suspended if he is on the court (17:3c), but disqualified if he is outside the court (substitutes and suspended players - 17:5c).

In the event of unsporting conduct or assault during an interruption of the game or time out, the game shall be restarted with the throw corresponding to the reason for the interruption.

17:12 Unsporting conduct or assault in the sport shall is to be penalized as follows:

Before the game:

a) A warning shall be given in the case of unsporting conduct (17:1d);
b) Pronounced unsporting conduct or assault shall be punished by disqualification (17:5d, f), but the team is allowed to start with 12 players;

During half-time:

c) A warning shall be given in the case of unsporting conduct (17:1d);
d) Repeated or pronounced unsporting conduct or assault shall be punished by disqualification (17:5c, d, f);

After the game:

e) A written report.

Rule 18 The Referees

18:1   Two referees with equal authority shall be in charge of each game. They shall be assisted by a score-taker and a time-keeper.

18:2   The referees monitor the conduct of the players from the moment they enter the premises until they leave.

18:3   The referees are responsible for examining the playing court, the goals, and the balls, prior to a game (3:1). They decide which ball shall be used. In the case of a disagreement, the opinion of the referee who is officially named first shall prevail.

The referees also establish the presence of both teams in the prescribed clothing, check the scoring sheet and players' equipment, check the manning of the substitution area, and in addition they establish the presence and identity of the officials appointed to be responsible for their teams.

Any discrepancies must be put straight (4:7).

18:4   The referee who is officially named first shall toss the coin before the game in the presence of the other referee and both team captains (10:1).

18:5   At the start of the game, the second named referee shall take up the position as court referee behind the team taking the throw-off, in their half of the court.

The court referee starts the game with a whistle signal for the throw-off (10:3).

When the other team gains possession of the ball, the second named referee takes up the position as goal line referee in his half of the court

The other referee starts as goal line referee at the other outer goal line and becomes the court referee when the team on his side gains possession of the ball.

The referees must change ends with each other from time to time during the game.

18:6   In principle, a game shall be conducted by the same two referees.

It is their joint responsibility to ensure that the game is played in accordance with the rules and they must penalize infringements, (see, however, 13:6, 14:9).

If either of the referees is unable to finish the game, the other referee should continue the game on his own.

18:7   The court referee principally whistles for:

a) taking a throw-off (10:3);
b) taking a penalty (14:2);
c) taking all throws according to the rules 16:3 b-h and after time out (18:11).

The goal-line referees shall blow his whistle:

d) when a goal has been scored (9:1).

18:8   If both referees make simultaneous decisions about penalizing the same team, but have different opinions as to which penalty should be given, the more severe penalty shall be enforced.

18:9   If both referees interrupt the game simultaneously, but have contradictory opinions as to which team should be penalized, the opinion of the court referee shall prevail.

Following clear hand signals from the court referee, the game is re-started by a whistle signal (16:3h).

18:10   Both referees are responsible for keeping the score. They shall also make notes of warnings, suspensions, disqualifications and exclusions.

18:11   Both referees are responsible for watching (controlling) the playing time. If there is any disagreement about the accuracy of the time-keeping, the referee who is officially named first decides on the correct time.

18:12   After the game the referees are responsible for a correct completion of the score sheet.

Disqualifications outside the court or after infringements against the referees, and exclusions must be explained on the score sheet (17:5d, f, 17:7).

18:13   Decisions made by the referees on the basis of their observation of the facts are final.

Appeals may be made against decisions which are not in accordance with the rules.

During the game only the team captains are allowed to address to the referees.

18:14   Both referees have the right to suspend a game temporarily or to call it off.

However, every effort shall be made to continue the game before a decisions taken to call it off.

18:15   The all black uniform is reserved for referees.

Rule 19 The Score-Taker and the Time-Keeper

19:1   The score-taker checks the team lists (only the players listed are entitled to participate) and, together with the time-keeper, the inclusion of players who have been suspended or who arrive after the game has started.

The score-taker is in charge of the score sheet and makes notes as appropriate (goals, warnings, suspensions, disqualifications and exclusions).

19:2   The time-keeper keeps control over:

a)   the playing time (2:1, 2, 4, 7; the referees decide when the clocks are to be stopped and re-started);
b)   the number of players and officials on the substitutes' benches (4:1);
c)   players who arrive late to make up the team, in collaboration with the score-taker (4:3);
d)   the exit and entry of substitutes (4:4-5);
e)   the entering of players not entitled to do so (4:6);
f)   the suspension time of players (17:4).

19:3   When there has been an interruption to the playing time (time-out), the time-keeper shall inform the responsible team officials how much time has been played and how much time remains (except when a clock is used which is publicly visible)

19:4   The time-keeper shall inform the suspended player or the responsible team official when the suspension time expires (17:4).

19:5   If the immediate result of a throw is to be awaited for (2:5), the time-keeper shall give the final signal:

a)   if the ball is thrown into the goal without any foul, when it is unimportant whether the ball has touched the goal-posts, the cross-bar, goal-keeper or a court player of the defending team;
b)   if the ball does not go into the goal or if it is passed.

Fouls committed before or during the taking of a free-throw or a penalty must be penalized and the final signal is then delayed further.

NOTES ON THE RULES OF THE GAME

Valid effective August 1989
Edition 1985

These Notes on the Rules of the Game as approved by the Council on July 1, 1988 replace all previous editions.

Editor: **INTERNATIONAL HANDBALL FEDERATION**
Lange Gasse 10
CH-4052 BASLE
Switzerland

1. Time-keeper's final signal (2:2, 2:5, 19:5)

At the end of a period of play the time-keeper ends the game with a clear signal. An automatic final signal may not be used. The time-keeper must concentrate fully on the clock, but also keep an eye on the game, so that he does not give the signal when the referees have just awarded a free-throw or penalty (2:5).

The score-taker shall watch the official clock for the last few seconds of play and count out loud the final seconds (55, 56, 57, 58, 59, finish) and the time-keeper shall watch the game only and give the final signal, if the game is not interrupted by the referees for a free-throw or a penalty beforehand.

The court referee must remain near the time-keeper's table during the last few seconds of each half so that he can always hear the final signal. If the goal referee, whose job it is to decide a goal, does not hear the final signal, the court referee shall decide whether a goal shot at the last moment shall be counted or not. (If necessary the time-keeper shall be consulted.)

If a free-throw or a penalty has been awarded the time-keeper must wait for the immediate result of the throw before giving the final signal. Immediate result in this case means as long as the ball is still moving under the impulse of the throw-in question. For example, the ball can, after a free-throw, touch the defence, bounce off the bar, hit the goal-keeper's back and then go into the goal.

2. "Time out" (2:4)

When should playing time be interrupted?

2.1   As a matter of principle in the case of:

    a)   outside influences, (e.g. spectators and objects on the court, damage to the goal or ball, ball under the stand, water on the court, power cut etc.);

    b)   disqualification or exclusion;

c) necessary consultations with the partner, score-taker/time-keeper;
d) suspected injuries (e.g. ball hits head).

2.2 As occasion demands in the case of:

e) delays in the taking of throws;
f) warning or suspensions;
g) substitution of the goal-keeper for penalty-throw;
h) faulty substitution or additional entering to the court;
i) throwing away or not giving the ball.

3. Unwarranted whistle signal from the timekeeper (2:6)

An unjustified blowing of the whistle results in a disadvantage for the team whose players were in possession of the ball.

The precise interpretation of the terms,, in possession of the ball" or,, a clear chance of getting in possession of the ball" shall be decided by the referees (factual decision).

The game shall be resumed according to rules 13:7 and 14:1a.

4. Disqualification and 2-minute suspension (4:3)

If a player not eligible to play is disqualified, a suspension is also imposed, this means that the number of players on the court is reduced.

5. Discrepancy between name and number (4:1, 4:3, 4:7)

If a player enters the court with a different number as the one allocated to him on the match report, the discrepancy has to be corrected according to the respective regulations. This infringement must be noted in the match report.

A disqualification or suspension shall not be given for this infringement.

6. Suspension time for "another player" (4:3, 4:6)

If "another player" has to leave the court instead of a guilty player to cover a complete or partial suspension time, this "other player" shall remain fully eligible for action and may again be substituted during this time.

The suspension time must be attributed only to the guilty player on the match report.

7. Observance of the substitution line (4:4, 3rd paragraph)

If permission is given after ,,time-out" to enter the court (4.4. referee's signal 18) the observance of the substitution line is not required.

No additional punishment shall be pronounced if a suspended player does not observe the substitution line while leaving the court. (Exception: unsporting conduct.)

8. Substitution of the goal-keeper for a penalty (4:4, 4th paragraph)

It is not permitted to change the goal-keeper after the thrower of the penalty is ready to throw in the right position with the ball in his hand.

If, however, the goal-keeper in this sitution does attempt a substitution, he shall be warned for ,,unsporting conduct" according to rule 17:1d and must remain in the goal.

If, nevertheless, he insists on substitution he shall be suspended for ,,repeated unsporting conduct".

He shall be suspended as well if he has already been warned or if his team has already received three warnings.

Whether the goal-keeper has been told by his trainer to change or not is irrelevant.

9. Two faults while substitution (4:4 comments)

If both, the entering and the exiting player, make a mistake while substitution, the player who first made a fault will be penalized.

10. Faulty substitution or faulty entering during a clear chance of scoring (4:5, 4:6)

If, during a clear chance of scoring, a faulty substitution is made by the team which is not in possession of the ball or an additional player enters the court and the score-taker/time keeper interrupt the game thereupon, a penalty-throw shall be awarded.

11. Illegal intereference with the game (4:6)

If a player from the substitution area touches the ball on the playing court he shall be punished the same as an additional player who interferes with the game against the rules.

12. Headbands (4:7)

Headbands are allowed for confining long hair as long as they are made of stretchy material (e.g. jersey, wool etc.)

13. Repeated entering of the goal area (6:2b)

If a defending player enters without the ball the goal area repeatedly in more or less the same circumstances, this behaviour shall be regarded as ,,unsporting conduct" (warning, 2-minute suspension, etc.). The player shall be cautioned before any punishment for "unsporting conduct" is imposed.

14. Entering the goal area during a clear chance of scoring (6:2b, 14:1a)

The attacking player is waiting outside the goal area line for the ball which has bounced off the goal-keeper or the goal. The defending player has no chance of getting the ball without infringing the rules. To avoid the chance of a goal being scored the defending player enters the goal area and prevents the attacking player from getting the ball.

If the referees are sure in this special case that a clear chance of scoring has been spoiled deliberately by the defending player entering the goal area, penalty-throw must be awarded.

15. Fumbling (7:7)

Exemption from penalisation for fumbling can only be given if the ball has just been received from another player.

For example, fumbling shall be punished if the ball is brought under control and after bouncing or dribbling is touched more than once.

16. Progressive punishmnent (8:13, 17:1b, 17:5e)

Progressive punishment means that a foul against an opponent exceeds the more common types of infringement which occur repeatedly in the struggle for the ball, and that the foul therefore shall not be penalised with only a free-throw.

Actions directed mainly or exclusively at the opponent and not the ball should lead to progressive punishment assuming that the actions fall under rules 8:4-11. These are mainly the straightforward fouls: grabbing, holding, pushing, running or jumping into, tripping, and hitting the opponent.

Action directed exclusively at the opponent as laid out in rule 8:3 is, of course, allowed.

If a foul is to be progressively penalised, this means that a warning is to be given the first time, and that each successive occurrence should be more severely punished, up to disqualification. Warnings or suspensions for other reasons (standing too close, not giving the ball etc.) are also to be included in the escalation up to the disqualification, as are punishments for "unsporting conduct".

17. Unsporting conduct (8:13, 17:1d)

Unsporting conduct can be:

a) shouting or calling when an opponent takes a penalty-throw;
b) during timeout: if a player from the team taking a free-throw goes to take the ball and the opponent kicks it away at the last moment;
c) abusing opponents and each other;
d) when a substitute player will not give back the ball when it lands over the side lines;
e) delay of a throw;
f) holding an opponent by his clothing;
g) penalty: the goal-keeper requires time-out for goal-keeper for substitution, goes to the substitution area and then returns back to the goal;
h) penalty-throw: the goal-keeper does not release the ball;
i) repeated defence with lower leg or foot by the player.

18. Serious infringements of the rules (8:14, 17:5b)

Serious infringements can be:

a) obvious pulling back of a thrower's arm while he is throwing, without any recognisable attempt at getting ball;
b) hitting an opponent during defensive action;
c) holding or pulling down a counter-attacking player in possession of the ball;
d) pushing an opponent who is taking a jumping-shot, without any recognisable attempt at getting the ball;
e) deliberate tripping;
f) if the goal-keeper who is not moving is hit on his head by a penalty-throw.

19. Pronounced unsporting conduct (8:14, 17:5d)

Pronounced unsporting conduct can be:

a) offences against the referees;
b) goal-keeper or player throwing or pushing the ball away after a referee's decision;

c) penalty: the goal-keeper takes a passive attitude, e.g. leans against the post and gives the impression of not wanting to take the penalty;
d) reflex action after a foul (hitting back);
e) deliberately throwing the ball at an opponent after the game is stopped or the playing time is interrupted (can also include assault);
f) if an additional player or an official spoils a clear chance of scoring.

20. Assault (8:15, 17:7)

To spit at somebody is equal to an assault; therefore an exclusion must be pronounced.

21. Delaying the throw-off (10:4)

If the throw-off, after a goal is scored, is delayed, this is to be regarded as "unsporting conduct".

In judging the facts of the case the tactical advantage of the situation must also be considered.

Examples:
a) To delay the throw-off, the goal scorer stays in the opponent's half longer than necessary to delay the correct positioning for a throw-off according to the rules.
b) To prevent the opponents catching up after scoring a goal — as in the case of a draw — the ball is returned to the middle of the court only after considerable delay.

22. No throw-in (11:1)

If a player happens to go outside the court in running after or trying to get the ball — as long as the ball does not cross the side lines or outer goal lines — the game shall continue.

If, however, a player gains an unfair advantage simply by going off te court, a free-throw must be awarded to the opponents.

23. Position for taking a free-throw (13:2)

In principle a free-throw should be taken from the place where the foul was committed.

If an opponent infringes rule 17:3d (not putting down the ball when a decision is taken against the team in possession of the ball), the player at fault is to be penalised with suspension and the free-throw shall be taken from the place where the foul was committed.

In other cases it is permitted to take the free-throw from where the ball is positioned, provided this is not further than about 3 metres from the place of the foul and is near the team's own goal area. The nearer the free-throw is to the opponent's free-throw line, the smaller the distance allowed.

24. Putting down of the ball (13:8)

When the referee blows his whistle against the team in control of the ball, the player in possession of the ball must immediately put or drop the ball on the ground without putting any force or direction behind it.

If the whistle must be blown again in context with this fault, the player shall be suspended.

This suspension without a prior warning due to non-releasing the ball by the team in possession of it, applies to free-throw, throw-in and goal-throw.

25. Infringing to spoil a clear chance of scoring (14:1a)

Infinging to spoil a clear chance of scoring a goal by anybody who is not involved in the game can be:

a) intereference with a player who has a clear opportunity to score a goal;
b) being present on the court, which prevents the real opportunity of scoring a goal;
c) catching or playing away of the ball which had been played in the direction of a player who was in a position to have a direct opportunity to score.

26. Referee's throw (15:3)

The two players jumping for the ball shall stand beside the referee, one each side, and not in front of him, to avoid premature body contact between the opponents.

The players may face whichever way they like (depending on which leg they jump off from).

The referee shall step back a little bit after throwing the ball up.

27. Throws from the wrong position (16:1)

If a throw which is to be taken without any signal from the referee, is taken from the wrong place, the referees have to correct the position and continue the game with a signal.

If it can be seen that such a throw is taken from the wrong place with the aim of gaining time, this shall be regarded as ,,unsporting conduct" (17:1d or 17:3c). Then the game is to be resumed with the appropriate throw after the referee's signal. It is recommended to give time out.

28. Leaving the substitution area after disqualification or exclusion (17:5, 17:6, 17:7)

Officials and players who have to leave the substitution area because they were disqualified or excluded, are not permitted to give any further instructions to their teams. They must keep away from locations from where they could influence their teams.

29. Note regarding direct disqualification (17:5b, d)

The PRC/IHF points out once again, that disqualification for ,,serious infingement of the rules" or ,,extreme unsportsmanlike conduct" is in principle a punishment for the remainder of the current game only. It is to be regarded as a factual decision by the referee and no other consequences should follow (except in the case of offending the referees).

30. Disqualification on the court (17:5, 17:12)

Offences which take place on the court before the game or during the intermission and which result in a disqualification, shall not lead to a 2-minute suspension.

31. Interrupting the game (18:14)

If the game has been interrupted by a referee's decision and a player or official cautioned or penalised, the game must be resumed with a free-throw from the position of the infringement — penalty, if a clear chance of scoring a goal was spoiled — by the opposing team.

If the game is interrupted by the scoretaker/timekeeper, the game shall be resumed with the throw corresponding to the game situation at the time of the interruption (except in cases of faulty substitution).

32. End of suspension time (19:4)

It is recommended—especially to avoid any problems because of language differences in international games — that the end of the suspension time, i.e. the time that a player can re - enter the court, is written down on a piece of paper and shown promptly to the team official.

SUBSTITUTION AREA REGULATIONS

1. The substitution areas are situated to the left and right of a continuation of the centre line, up to 1.5 m outside the side line and also behind the substitution benches if space allows (Rules of the Game: figure 1).

   Nothing of any description whatsoever may be allowed to stand near the side lines throughout the outer end of the substitution benches (at least 8 m from the centre line).

2. Only the players and officials entered on the scoring sheet may be allowed to stay in the substitution area (rule 4:1).

   If an interpreter is necessary, he must take up his position behind the substitution bench.

   Players and officials who wish to leave the substitution area, must inform the score-taker/time-keeper through the team official responsible when they leave and when they return.

3. The officials of a team in the substitution area must be fully dressed in sports wear or civilian clothing.

4. The score-taker/time-keeper shall support the referees in seeing that the substitution area is correctly used before and during the game.

   If, before the game, there are any infringements of the rules as regards the substitution area, the game may not start until they have been straightened out. If such rules are infringed during a game, the game may not be continued after the next interruption until they have been rectified.

5. The officials have the right and duty to guide and tend their team in a fair and sporting spirit within the framework of the rules during the game.

   Both officials and players who are in the substitution area must sit on the substitution bench.

5.1 It is, however, permitted to stand up briefly:
   a) when a player is substituted;
   b) to give advice on tactics to players on the court and on the bench;
   c) to give medical care;
   d) to warm up, without a ball, behind the substitution bench, if there is sufficient room and does not cause any disturbance;
   e) to speak to the score-taker/time-keeper (this only applies to the official responsible for tht team in unusual situations, see rule 4:1).

5.2   It is not permitted:
        a) to stand or to move for an extended period of time in front
            of or near the bench in a disturbing manner;
        b) for players or officials to produce a hampering or insulting effect
            on referees, score-taker/time-keeper, players, officials or spec-
            tators in a provoking or protesting manner (by speech, mime
            or gestures);
        c) to leave the substitution area on the side line to influence the
            course of the game;
        d) to stand or move on the side line while warming up.

6.   If the substitution area regulations are infringed, the referees are
        obliged to act according to rules 17:1d or 17:5d (warning, disquali-
        fication).

7.   If the referees fail to notice an infringement of the substitution area
        regulations, they must be informed of it by the score-taker/time-
        keeper or the IHF representative during the next interruption of the
        game.

ATTACHMENTS

A. Classification in World Championships
B. Classification in the European Cup Competition
**C. Matters not provided for and urgent cases at official
IHF-events**

A.   Classification in World Championships
(Extract of the ,,World Championship Regulations")

**5.   Classification in the preliminary, main and classification
        rounds**

5.1.   The matches in the preliminary, main and classification rounds will
        consist of two periods of 30 minutes each with an interval of 10
        minutes at half-time, without extra time. The score will be evaluated
        as follows:

        – match won   2 points
        – match tied   1 point for each team
        – match lost   0 points

5.2.   Classification of teams is made in each round by adding together
        the points gained.

5.3.   If two or more teams have gained the same number of points, the
        teams which have gained at least 25% of the points possible and
        the teams which have gained less than 25% of the points possible
        will be evaluated separately.

5.4.   The order of classification criteria is as follows:
- higher goal difference calculated by subtraction
- higher number of goals scored result(s) of match(es) played between the teams concerned.

5.5.   If classification is still not possible, the following items will decide:
- the goal difference in all the games together
- the higher total number of goals scored in all matches played.

5.6.   If classification is still not possible, it will be decided by lot. Lots will be drawn on the spot by the IHF representative, if possible in the presence of representatives of the teams concerned.

6.   Classification in the final rounds

6.1.   In drawn matches in the final round—after an intermission of 5 minutes—a first period of extra time of 2x5 minutes without interval with change of ends will be played.

6.2.   If the match is still not decided, after an intermission of 5 minutes, a second period of extra time of 2x5 minutes with change of ends without interval will be played.

6.3.   If the winner is still not obtained the match will be decided by penalty throws, as follows:

6.3.1.   For the penalty throws each team shall nominate five eligible players who take it in turns with their opponents to throw once each. A list of the names and numbers of the throwers has to be handed in to the referees. The five players may throw in any order.

6.3.2.   The goalkeepers may be chosen and changed at will.

6.3.3.   The referees shall decide which goal is to be used and toss for the team to start.

6.3.4.   If the game is undecided after the first round of throws, five chosen players (eitehr the same five players, or a change of one to five players on a new list) shall continue to throw until a result is achieved. The teams shall take turns to start. "Until a result is achieved" in this case means: (1) if for example the team throwing first fails to score, the other team must score to win, and (2) if the team throwing first scores and the other fails to score, the first team wins.

    The same system will be followed up until a decision is reached.

6.3.5.   Players who have been sent off, disqualified, or excluded are not allowed to throw penalties.

6.3.6.   Bad conduct during the penalty throw shall be punished without exception by disqualification. If a player is disqualified or injured an eligible substitute must be nominated.

6.3.7   While penalties are being thrown, only the player taking the throw, the defending goalkeeper and the referees may be on the half of the court being used.

B.   Classification in the European Cup Competition
(Extract of the ,,Regulations for European Competitions")

4.   Classification

4.1.   Classification will be made by adding points as follows:
win   = 2 points
draw   = 1 point
defeat   = 0 points

4.2   If two teams have the same number of points after both home and away match, classification will be made on the following grounds:
a)   goal difference
b)   higher number of goals scored in away match
c)   by means of penalty throws (without previous extra time).

4.3.1.   If penalty throws are necessary, each team shall nominate five eligible players who take it in turns with their opponents to thow once each. A list of the names and numbers of the throwers has to be handed in to the referees. The five players may throw in any order.

4.3.2.   The goalkeepers may be chosen and changed at will.

4.3.3.   The referees shall decide which goal is to be used and toss for the team to start.

4.3.4.   If the game is undecided after the first round of throws, five chosen players (either the same five players, or a change of one to five players on a new list) shall continue to throw until a result is achieved. The teams shall take turns to start. ,,Until a result is achieved" in this case means: (1) if for example the team throwing first fails to score, the other team must score to win, and (2) if the team throwing first scores and the other fails to score, the first team wins.

The same system will be following up until a decision is reached.

4.3.5.   Players who have been sent off, disqualified, or excluded are not allowed to throw penalties.

4.3.6.   Bad conduct during the penalty throws shall be punished without exception by disqualification. If a player is disqualified or injured an eligible substitute must be nominated.

4.3.7.   While penalities are being thrown, only the player taking the throw, the defending goalkeeper and the referees may be on the half of the court being used.

in the case of one final only the result is a draw even after two periods of extra time, according to the IHF playing rules, the match shall be replayed in the same country within two days. If it is still drawn even after extra time, a decision shall be reached by the system detailed under item 4.2.c.

C. Matters not provided for and urgent cases at official IHF-events (Extract from the ,,IHF-Statues", section 53.2)

53.2   In case of unforeseen incidents (power cuts, riots, acts of God, etc.) the match shall be played to the end if at all possible (with or without public). If the match cannot be continued, it shall be continued the day after (same result, reamining time of play) either by a throw-on to be taken by the team that was last in possession of the ball, or by a referee's throw (Rules of the Game 13:7, 15:1 c).

The right to decide rests with an official IHF representative, if present. Otherwise, the referees shall decide.